The Devon Almanac

THE
MINT
PRESS

The Devon
Almanac

Todd Gray

THE MINT PRESS

For Ian

First published in Great Britain by The Mint Press, 2000

ISBN 1-903356-01-6

British Library Cataloguing-in-Publication Data
A CIP record for this title is available from
the British Library

The Mint Press
18 The Mint
Exeter, Devon
England, EX4 3BL

Designed and typeset in New Baskerville 10.5/13.5
by Mike Dobson

Cover design by Delphine Jones

Main cover illustration 'Guy Fawkes Night' by A.P., *The Pictorial World*,
4th November 1882, by courtesy Westcountry Studies Library

Printed and bound in Great Britain
by Short Run Press Ltd, Exeter.

CONTENTS

Planting the village Maypole

Editorial Notes

The material for this book comes from a wide variety of printed sources, notably including eighteenth and nineteenth-century newspapers held at the Devon & Exeter Institution and Westcountry Studies Library, and manuscript sources mostly held in the Devon Record Office, North Devon Record Office and the Plymouth and West Devon Record Office.

Acknowledgements

I am grateful to Ian Maxted, Mrs Margery Rowe, John Draisey and the staff of the Devon Record Office, the staff of the Westcountry Studies Library, in particular Tony Rouse, and Madeleine Midgely of the Devon & Exeter Institution for help during the preparation of this volume.

The illustrations for each month are derived from William Hone, *Every-day Book* (1825), in two volumes. References for all other illustrations, which appear by the kind permission of the Westcountry Studies Library, are listed on pages 207 to 209.

Ah! You April Fool!

MOVEABLE DATES

Shrove Sunday (Quinquagesima)

Collop Monday

Shrove-Tuesday / Pancake Day (Tuesday following Quinquagesima Sunday – falling between February 2nd and March 8th)

Ash Wednesday (First of the 40 days of Lent)

Lent (40 days of appropriate denial)

Passion Sunday (5th Sunday in Lent)

Passion Week (Week after Palm Sunday)

Palm Sunday (6th Sunday in Lent)

Maundy Thursday (Thursday before Good Friday)
   Peter's Pence was traditionally given at Exeter Cathedral

Good Friday (Friday before Easter Sunday)

Easter (ranging from 22nd March to 25th April – Sunday after full moon or after 21st March)

Hock Day collection of money for charity (2nd Tuesday after Easter)

Rogation Sunday (5th Sunday after Easter Day)

Rogation Days – the time of parish perambulations (Monday, Tuesday, Wednesday before Ascension Day)

Ascension Day (Thursday following Rogation Sunday)

Whit Sunday / Pentecost (7th Sunday after Easter Day)

Whitsuntide (Whit-Sunday, -Monday, -Tuesday)

Trinity Sunday (Sunday following Pentecost)

Trinity Tuesday (Tuesday following Trinity Sunday)

Corpus Christi (Thursday following Trinity Sunday)

The Devon Almanac

For sports, for pageantry and plays
    Thou hast thy eves and holidays;
On which the young men and maids meet
    To exercise their dancing feet;
Tripping the comely country round,
    With daffodils and daisies crown'd.
Thy wakes, thy quintals here thou hast,
    Thy May-poles, too, with garlands grac'd;
Thy Morris dance, thy Whitsun ale;
    Thy shearing feast which never fail;
Thy harvest home, thy wassail bowl,
    That's toss'd up after fox i' th' hole;
Thy mummeries, thy Twelfth-tide kings
    And queens, thy Christmas revellings,
Thy nut-brown mirth, thy russet wit,
    And no man pays too dear for it.

Robert Herrick, Rector of Dean Prior,
1629 to 1647 and 1662 to 1674

JANUARY

When Christmas is ended, bid feasting adieu,
go play the good husband, thy stock to renew,
Be mindful of rearing, in hope of a gain,
dame profit shall give thee reward for thy pain.

Thomas Tusser, 1557

JANUARY

❧ 1 ❦

1635 An anonymous writer suggested ransoming the Barbary pirates' captives, many of whom were from Devon, with English 'harlots & the idle & the lascivious portion of the female sex...so one harlot might redeem half a dozen captives'.

1772 A Crediton woman poisoned herself and an Exeter woman hanged herself in a doorway in Northgate Street.

1824 Plymouth Dock was officially renamed Devonport.

1839 More than 360 people at Exeter's Race Fund Ball enjoyed a Quadrille Band with mulled wine 'besides the usual tea and other refreshments'.

1847 A home-grown cucumber measuring 21 inches, was sliced by Mr Hodge, a Sidmouth surgeon.

1867 At Torquay more than 1,000 workers marched in support of Reform.

1876 For a New Year's Treat children were given toys and sweets, women had tea and sugar, and men had tobacco at the Newton Abbot Union Workhouse.

1901 The editor of *The Devon and Exeter Gazette* asked 'Are our hopes of the New Year, the first of the Twentieth Century, well founded? We think we may expect much as a nation. We have a great past; we may reasonably hope for a glorious future. What we have done we can do again – and do better. A nation can renew its strength, and thus be over ready to add to its achievements. The British people have a history of which they are not ashamed. We believe the chapter now opened will be a worthy addition'.

1904 The first registration of cars in Exeter recorded 12 motor vehicles in the city.

1915 The crew of the *Provident*, Brixham trawler, rescued 71

❄❄❄ *Gardening advice from* The South Molton Almanack ❄ 1891 – *When the frost is not intense, trench, manure, and turn up all vacant ground in*

JANUARY

survivors of HMS *Formidable*, sunk in the Channel by German submarines.

❧ 2 ❦

1591   Burial of John Bartlett, Exeter's Sword Bearer, who walked before the Mayor carrying the sword given by Henry VII.

1767   Two lions, a tiger and an 'Egyptian' hyena, which reportedly imitated human voices 'by which means he decoys the Negroes from their huts and then devours them', were on show in Exeter.

1827   Bideford Bridge was about to be lit by twelve lamps.

1930   A political cartoon in *The Devon & Exeter Gazette* showed the New Year Baby summoning nations to the London Naval Conference.

❧ 3 ❦

1629   The week's expenses at Forde House in Newton Abbot included 10 rabbits, a side of mutton, 12 snipes, a quart of tar, 4 cocks and 2 quarts of mustard seed.

1826   A con man (five feet eight inches high, swarthy complexion, mustachios, wearing a brown frock coat and blue pantaloons) feigned being a survivor of a Teignmouth shipwreck to swindle donations from local gentry.

1829   Death of Elizabeth Blanchard of Exeter, an 'antiquated female remarkable during her life for ready wit and rhyme', at the age of one hundred years.

1848   Matthew Lowe, former servant of Admiral Sir John West, was apprehended in Manchester with fifteen diamonds recently stolen from Miss Harriet Sophia Smith and Miss Jane West of Devonport.

ridges. Prepare hotbeds. Plant, prune, and train standard and wall fruit-trees, raspberry, gooseberry, and current bushes. Edge beds, construct new flower

JANUARY

❧ 4 ❧

1609 The *Rosemary* of Topsham arrived from Rochelle with a cargo of vinegar.

1816 It was reported that lead coffins had been uncovered in Plymouth containing the remains of two naval captains shot for cowardice 95 years before.

1844 A 2½ year-old Newfoundland dog from Otterton was offered for sale, being a 'handsome, large thoroughbred...of perfect symmetry and great activity...a capital animal for house or road'.

1882 The Plymouth Cooperative Society announced an annual profit of £13,000.

❧ 5 ❧

1669 Agnes Truss, a widow of St Sidwell's parish, who was reputedly 100 years old, was buried.

1839 Two Exeter women, Sarah Squiers and Charlotte Dawe alias Charlotte Mugford, were convicted of enticing a man into their house and stealing his purse containing a sovereign, silk handkerchief and knife.

1877 The editor of *The Devon Weekly Times* noted the New Year had begun dismally with extreme wet weather threatening disease and 'physically and politically we are shrouded with gloom'.

1877 A magic lantern show on the Prince of Wales' tour in India was held in Hatherleigh.

1916 Death of Harry Hems, noted Exeter sculptor, writer.

gardens, and shelter tulips, ranunculuses, and tender evergreens from frost.
✸ *1896 – Sow beans for transplanting in March; cabbage at the close of the*

JANUARY

❧ 6 ❧
Twelfth Day

1679 Prudence Baldwin, servant to Robert Herrick, poet, was buried at Dean Prior.

1819 It was reported from Plymouth that Archduke Maximilian of Austria had descended in the Diving Bell during a visit which had 'created some little bustle'.

1829 Exeter's confectioners decorated their shops one with 'tasteful evergreens and variegated lamps interspersed' and another was emblematic showing 'cavalry and infantry mounted on the huge frost covered hills of plum and spice reminded us of Bonaparte and his army crossing the Alps'.

1899 Passage on the Orient Line from Plymouth to the West Australian Goldfields was advertised.

❧ 7 ❧
St Distaff's Day / Rock Day

1619 Burial of Nicholas Hilliard, Devon miniaturist, in London.

1829 A wag responded to the winter's interruption of gas lamps in the parish of St Thomas by writing:
> Like the regions infernal, divested of light,
> With much grief the sad change we remark;
> For since Peter and Paul, John and Sidwell, look bright,
> Why should Thomas be 'left in the dark?'

1839 G. Carter, Exeter optician, offered Eye Preservers, 'Spectacles possessing all the qualities which fashion and real utility demand', at reduced London prices.

1845 The editor of *Beasley's Devonshire Chronicle and Exeter News* informed his readers that the dance steps of the polka imitated the Polish peasants in 'kicking the wet snow off their heels'.

1846 William Macready played Hamlet at Exeter.

month and peas on a sheltered border. The first interval of open weather should be taken advantage of to get in any bulbs which may remain unplanted. Train

JANUARY

❧ 8 ❧

1672 Plymouth's mayor ordered that pigs were not to stray within the streets and 'heaps of dung, filth or rubbish' should not lay in public places for more than 24 hours.

1767 The *Fanny* of Bideford arrived in Exeter with a cargo of Irish beef and butter.

1827 Many Exeter shops closed in mourning the Duke of York.

1877 A rabid spaniel bit several inhabitants of Wivelscombe.

❧ 9 ❧

1539 Henry Courtenay, earl of Devon, was executed for treason.

1659 John Wood of Plymouth was accused of missing church in order to go walking on the Hoe.

1666 Misdemeanants at Dartmouth included Oliver Hawkes for being drunk and swearing nine times, Ursula Abraham for being pregnant with an illegitimate child, two men for not attending church services and two others for drinking at a 'disorderly hour'.

1769 A young man was whipped at Exeter for stealing a cock and hen.

1990 It was announced in London that 9 cattle recently slaughtered in Devon & Cornwall were found to carry BSE.

❧ 10 ❧

1814 (10th–11th) A heavy snowstorm hit Devon.

1816 A Plymouth man, who reputedly worked 'in the mystic art of Necromancy', was committed to gaol.

1816 The death of Mr William Humphreys of Cowley Bridge was reported in *The Exeter Flying Post*.

neatly creepers, such as honeysuckle, rose, vine, and clematis. Mignonette, stocks &c. should be sown in pots, and sweet peas, and a few hardy annuals on a

JANUARY

1845 Mr Halls, Professor of Dancing, gave an evening of entertainment at the Globe Hotel in Newton Abbot – a series of continental dances, mainly Polkas, were performed by his daughters 'with much elegance and taste' for 'the very respectable audience'.

1866 Damage from a snowstorm included 30 vessels wrecked in Torbay and thousands of trees lost.

1924 The Association of West Countrymen in Folkestone held their annual Children's Party.

❧ 11 ❦

1636 The curate of Brampford Speke was accused of visiting alehouses until 2 a.m. and of immorality with his parishioners.

1641 John Pentner of Alphington was alleged to have called his neighbour Joan Ridgeway a whore and a base whore.

1793 An effigy of Tom Payne was paraded through Exeter, hanged and burned.

1843 Arrangements were finalised by James Veitch, Exeter nurseryman, to send Thomas Lobb as a botanical collector on an expedition to Singapore, Java and China.

1875 A whale, 75 feet long, was sighted at Teignmouth.

1877 The outer wall of the old Exeter city prison was demolished in preparation for building the Rougemont Hotel.

❧ 12 ❦

Birthday of William Pengelly, 'father' of the Devonshire Association: born at East Looe, Cornwall, 1812.

1770 Two Okehampton cloth-makers insured their property for £500.

warm border. Protect choice bulbs against frost. ❄ 1898 – *In the beginning of this month sow early peas; early mazagan and long-pod peas during the first*

JANUARY

1793 Twelve crewmembers were lost in the wreck of a Dutch ship near Salcombe.

1608 Stephen Cockworthie of Malborough was whipped for stealing a hen and a goose. His punishment was in lieu of imprisonment because he was 'an unclean man with the leprosy and therefore not fit to be sent to the gaol'.

1771 The *St Joseph* of London was driven onto the sands at Paignton.

1828 A violent storm hit the county from the south west.

1829 It was reported that a youth, dressed in a sheet, rose from behind an Exeter grave in an attempt to frighten a servant girl and uttered 'I am a spirit rising from the tomb' to which she replied 'Then lie down again'.

1915 Believers in Joanna Southcott, visionary, were disappointed that on the centenary of her death her sealed prophecies were not called for 'suddenly and unaware in a time of national danger'.

1976 Death of Agatha Christie, writer.

❧ 13 ❧

1676 Three snuff dishes were purchased at Sydenham.

1816 Fire destroyed more than a dozen buildings in Moreton-hampstead.

1842 John Foulston, architect, died in Plymouth.

1843 A storm of thunder, lightning and snow hit Devon.

1880 Five inches of snow fell in Exeter at night.

1899 Messrs. Robert Veitch & Son advertised their new potato variety 'Devonian'.

and last weeks; onions in very light soils; parsley, short-topped radish, and hardy green and brown Dutch lettuce. Prune all kinds of fruit-trees. Sow salads,

JANUARY

1930   Appearing at the Exeter Hippodrome were The Greyhound Serenaders, Tom Wood and his saxophone, The Introduction Girls, Bernard Wells and his accordion, Moxham Brothers, trick cyclists, and Fred Brand, the 'Speed Man' with his feet.

1948   Casting began for *Dead Ground*, the first production of Oldway Film Studios in Paignton.

❧ 14 ❧
St Hilary's Day

1831   Jane Powesland, 51, stole 3¼ pounds of bacon from a Colyton shop for which she was later sentenced 6 months imprisonment at hard labour.

1835   Three woodlarks were heard singing in Yealmpton.

1839   The Telegraph day coach was expected to arrive at Pratt's Old London Inn, Exeter, from London in 15 hours, the Vivid coach in 17 hours from London and the York House in 9 hours from Bath.

1900   A county footballer was summoned before Barnstaple Police Court for 'furious driving': he was accused of crossing Long Bridge in a pony trap at the rate of nine to ten miles an hour.

❧ 15 ❧

1664   A five-foot long monster was reportedly swimming at Axmouth.

1871   A strong gale blew through Holsworthy.

1878   The weekly meeting of the Exeter Corporation of the Poor heard that there were 1,408 paupers and 20 vagrants.

carrots and kidney beans on slight hotbeds. Transplant herbaceous plants in light soils. Trim neatly roses and creeping plants. ❀ 1900 – *Protect choice plants.*

JANUARY

1930 An advert in *The Devon & Exeter Gazette* called for experienced farm families, domestic servants, single men and boys to emigrate to Canada.

❧ 16 ❦

1634 Householders in Exeter were ordered to keep light their doorways at night from November to January.

1646 The long Royalist siege of Plymouth ended.

1843 A premium of two pounds was given at the Totnes Agricultural Society's Ploughing Match to William Tinkham as a 'Labourer who has lived and worked the longest with one master' (49 years).

1847 It was reported that the daughter of a Barnstaple clergyman had eloped with a local lad who was 'of respectable but not equally good connections'. The two nineteen-year olds left a note implying they were fleeing to Ilfracombe but it transpired they escaped via the Exeter railway station.

1880 A solar halo was seen at Babbacombe from 10.30 to 11.30 in the morning.

❧ 17 ❦

1608 At Exeter 'by reason of an extreme frost which continued down the river of Exe such huge stacks of ice which rested upon our weir and so brake Collibear weir and likewise True's weir...to the great hurt of the city and citizens. It was so extreme that the like hath not been seen by any man now living amongst us'.

1816 *The Exeter Flying Post*'s report on January 10th of the death of Mr Humphreys of Cowley Bridge proved premature.

Train neatly vines, roses, clematis, honeysuckle. Water plants in pots sparingly. Sow cabbage towards the end of the month. Sow double-blossomed frame peas on

JANUARY

1870   A father and son travelling in a bread cart had a lucky escape when their horse bolted over the cliff at Hope Cove but neither horse nor the humans were fatally injured.

❧ 18 ❧

1837 (18th–21st)   Influenza was widespread and symptoms included oppressive head pains, constant sneezing and diffused muscular pains in the shoulders, loins and legs.

1845   It was rumoured that Mr I.K. Brunel would soon arrive in Tiverton to decide upon the railway station's location, an issue which had apparently divided local opinion.

1848   A hard frost delayed the first down train of the South Devon Railway.

1877   A company of minstrels played in Teignmouth.

1881 (18th–19th)   Heavy snow fell across England with as much as a foot falling in Exeter and Gittisham, 18 inches in Kingsbridge and 22 inches in Cullompton and Bradninch.

❧ 19 ❧

1804 (19th–20th)   A storm caused the loss of ten vessels off the Devon coast.

1829   It was reported in *The Alfred* that the County Meeting resolved that no further political concessions should be granted to Catholics.

1829   Mr William Burch, a former Exeter solicitor, 31 years old, 'fell a victim to the extreme sensibility of his nature arising from the unfortunate mental affliction of Mrs Burch'.

1880   At Exeter the river Exe froze over.

a sheltered border, but only if the weather is favourable. In open weather plant any bulbs, such as narcissus, anemones, and tulips, that remain unplanted.

JANUARY

1882 A Plymouth seaman was sentenced to five years penal servitude for striking a corporal.

❧ 20 ❧

1387 The gates into Cathedral Yard in Exeter were ordered to be closed at night.

1607 A great flood swept through Barnstaple.

1769 An Exeter woman stood for an hour in the pillory in front of the Guildhall for keeping a Disorderly House.

1792 A French lugger was driven onto Exmouth bar.

1804 Ilfracombe's vicar was found not guilty of brawling in church.

1827 The Reverend Moses Levy performed an additional service at the Jewish Synagogue as a mark of respect for the death of the Duke of York.

1930 Appearing at the Exeter Hippodrome were Fred Roper and his 'wonderful midgets'.

❧ 21 ❧

Astrological Sign of AQUARIUS, the Water Carrier
(through to February 19th)

1652 Jonathan Pickard, an orphan aged 6½ years old, began school as a boarder at Barnstaple.

1801 Horatio Nelson received the freedom of the borough of Plymouth.

1853 *Uncle Tom's Cabin* packed the theatre at Exeter.

1870 A 'rocket apparatus' was sent to Croyde in the hope it would save mariners' lives.

Protect choice sorts of bulbs from severe frosts and heavy rains. ❋ 1901 – *Sow beans for transplanting in March; cabbage at the close of the month and peas on*

JANUARY

❧ 22 ❧

1657   In the kitchen's store chamber at Sydenham were a quarter and a breast of mutton, a quarter of veal, 1 pound of butter, 80 eggs, 4 tongues, 3 udders, 1 breast of pork, 4 marrow bones, 1 bushel of wheat, 1 pullet pie and a lumber pie.

1875   An eel, twelve inches long, was found blocking the water pipes of the Clarence Hotel in Ilfracombe.

1875   Three small granite crosses were discovered during restoration work in the church of Widecombe-in-the-Moor.

1877   A pure-white Barn owl was killed near Exeter.

1880   The freezing of the river Exe extended from Exeter to Lympstone.

❧ 23 ❧

Birthday of Dorothy Elmhirst, patron of Dartington Hall: 1887, in Washington D.C.

1779   A man with a 'foreign aspect' was suspected of attempting to destroy Plymouth Dockyard by fire.

1781   Hedges were being removed at Saltram in order to improve the viewing of the grounds.

1816   An inquest was held into the death of Jeremiah Lightholder, found dead in his Exeter privy.

1885   A former Exeter mayor complained of the foul language used by men and boys driving cattle through the streets.

1900   George Rowledge of Woodbury was fined 7s 2d for riding a bicycle on the footpath at Topsham.

1913   A self-confessed black sheep of the family, who spent most of his earnings on drink and 'amusements', was admitted to Exeter's hospital for drinking carbolic acid.

a sheltered border. The first interval of open weather should be taken advantage of to get in any bulbs which may remain unplanted. Train neatly creepers, such

JANUARY

❧ 24 ❧

Birthday of Benjamin R. Haydon, artist: born at Plymouth, 1786.

1390 An Exeter canon agreed to pay for the glazing of a window in the Cathedral's cloisters if he misbehaved again towards the Dean.

1793 The 'Amazing Pig of Knowledge', 'the most striking curiousity ever seen or heard of', was on view in Stonehouse.

1848 At Exeter William Smith, 'a young man of Barnstaple', was charged, but not convicted, of begging whereas Daniel Sullivan, 'a sturdy Irishman', was convicted of the same crime and committed to one week's hard labour.

1902 The first meeting was held of the Devon Dumplings Cricket Club (set up along the lines of the Hampshire Hogs and Somerset Stragglers).

1990 The National Farmers Union assured consumers that British beef was 'safe to eat'.

❧ 25 ❧

1664 Henry Snowe, Ilfracombe butcher, petitioned for the right to sell meat during Lent to 'old, weak or sick people'.

1793 A comet was visible in the early hours of the evening.

1858 A Chulmleigh boy was sentenced to three months' imprisonment for stealing cheese.

1885 The new seed catalogue of Messrs. Lucombe Pince & Co. had a number of new varieties including 'the Negro' potato, a black potato reputedly having a flavour between an ordinary potato and a Spanish chestnut.

1913 Two trams collided in Queen's Street, Exeter.

as honeysuckle, rose, vine, and clematis. Mignonette, stocks &c. should be sown in pots, and sweet peas, and a few hardy annuals on a warm border. Protect

JANUARY

❧ 26 ❦

1717 The Exeter to London post bags, which had been stolen, were found in Thread Needle Street.

1792 A high tide caused great damage to warehouses throughout Plymouth.

1821 An explosion occurred in the powder works of the Royal Dockyard.

1824 It was reported that an Exeter printer working in Canton was about to give the Devon & Exeter Institution the 'Chinese Monstrosity', a man between four and five feet high with a 'male child adhering by the neck to his breast'.

1917 (26th–27th) A violent storm washed away Hallsands.

❧ 27 ❦

1651 John Lavers, Exeter worsted-comber, and Richard Langworthy of Newton St Cyres were overheard drinking a toast to 'the little boy in buff', an allusion presumably to Charles II then twenty years old.

1767 Arson was suspected in the destruction of a building belonging to a Crediton clothmaker.

1792 Death of William Hill of Croyland, sexton and former thatcher, who was reported to have been blind for more than 20 years but could dig graves 'with as much propriety and accuracy as many who can see'.

1819 Twin infants were left at two Exeter doorways.

1824 It was reported that the Clovelly customs officer seized 59 tubs of contraband spirits and at Appledore three pilots were drowned.

choice bulbs against frost ✿ 1907 – *When the frost is not intense, trench, manure, and turn up all vacant ground in ridges. In open and dry weather sow – choosing*

JANUARY

1829 Spotted evergreen privets, from five to six feet high, were being sold by James Turner, nurseryman of St David's Hill, Exeter.

1849 The first salmon of the season from the Exe was sold in Exeter Fish Market.

❧ 28 ❧

Birthday of Sabine Baring Gould, cleric, writer: born at Exeter, 1834.

1444 Enquiries were made into the robbery of the *Mighell* of Dartmouth as it sailed into Plymouth harbour.

1595 Early in the morning Sir Francis Drake died of dysentery on the island of Buena Ventura at the Isthmus of Panama and was reportedly buried at sea in a lead coffin to the 'doleful' notes of trumpets.

1767 A dog discovered an infant's body wrapped in cloth in a field near Northernhay in Exeter.

1870 Sir Stafford Northcote gave a lecture, to support able-bodied unemployed workmen of Exeter, on 'The Opening of the Suez Canal'.

1885 A correspondent to *The Exeter Flying Post* suggested that orange peels should not be thrown in the streets of Exeter, Exmouth, Dawlish, Torquay or Dartmouth because pedestrians could slip and fall.

1927 Devon's wettest day of 1927.

❧ 29 ❧

1601 Thomas Gribble was buried in Barnstaple, two months after drowning.

a mild exposure – a few early frame peas, common beans, lettuces, onions, carrots, short-topped radishes, curled parsley and spinach, shielding them from frost by

JANUARY

1841 The street lamps of Sandford were first lit with oil lamps.

1875 Laceworkers in Barnstaple were allowed to return to work on the condition that they abandoned their union.

1875 The African Civilization Society met in Exeter.

1883 Honiton had a third day of violence with protests against the Salvation Army: the 'Skeletonite Army' met the visitors at the train station, pelted them with stones and red and orange ochre, and the town remained in a state of uproar through the night.

☙ 30 ❧

1815 A four-year old Exmouth child drank from a boiling tea kettle and died within a few hours from burns.

1824 The Corporation of Exeter observed the death of Charles I with a church service.

1900 Professor Crocker appeared at the Victoria Hall in Exeter with his 'educated horses'.

☙ 31 ❧

1764 A man died in the collapse of a house in Alphington.

1815 A reward was offered for the return of a light brindled sheep dog from Silverton who answered to the name of Guard.

1834 A brood of sparrows hatched in a nest near Plymouth.

1842 Violets, crocuses, snow drops and heath bloomed in the garden of Rougemont House in Exeter.

1914 A Nepal tiger, shot by King George V, was reported *in situ* at the Royal Albert Memorial Museum.

mats or straw. In hot beds sow cauliflowers, cucumbers, melons, small salading and early cabbage. Plant, prune, and train standard and wall fruit trees. ✳✳✳

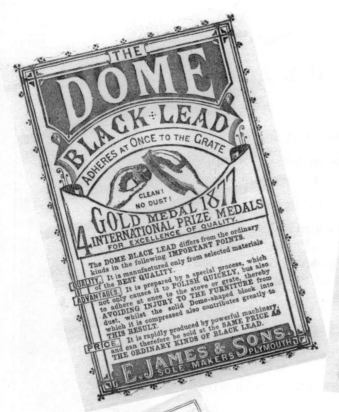

February

You have such a February face, so full of frost, of storm

William Shakespeare,
Much Ado about Nothing,
Act V, Scene 4

FEBRUARY

❧ 1 ❧
Candlemas Eve

1845 Two young boys were admonished by the Exeter Police for sliding in Cathedral Yard.

1870 Nearly three inches of rain fell on parts of Dartmoor.

1875 A bedridden old woman, who had formerly owned a cider shop but was currently being maintained at public expense, was discovered to own a bag in which she had hidden one hundred sovereigns.

1878 At Newton Abbot a lecture and demonstration were given on the telephone.

1913 *All Through a Turkey*, a comedy, played at Queen's Hall Pictures, Exeter.

❧ 2 ❧
Purification of the Virgin Mary / Candlemas

Birthday of Martin Dunsford, Tiverton historian: born at Tiverton, 1744

1803 It was reported that a rocking horse factory was being established in Exeter.

1824 The editor of *The Western Luminary* informed his readers the tide of opinion on slavery had turned and the sentiment 'Perish Mammon! Live Justice' was beginning to be heard.

1841 Barnardo Eagle, 'The Royal Eagle of the South', performed in Exeter showing 'Enchantments, photographic phenomena, cabalistic conjurations, mephistophelian transmutations'.

1901 A memorial service to mark Queen Victoria's death was held in Exeter Cathedral.

✸✸✸ 1896 – *Sow peas, the first favourable opportunity. Sow early long-pod beans for a main crop, and early radishes in a dry and sheltered situation. Plant*

FEBRUARY

❧ 3 ❧

1617 William Rugg of Newton Poppleford complained he was slandered by Thomasine Manly calling him a 'whoremaster knave'.

1768 Admission charges to view the collection of wild animals shown at Totnes were one shilling for those of 'a better sort' while the 'lower class' paid six pence.

1792 At the Customs House in Dartmouth 233 gallons of seized brandy, 195 of rum and 473 of 'Geneva' were auctioned.

1824 It was reported that the 'Metropolis of the West' had a 'rapid increase of new buildings' including Southernhay Place.

1866 Thunderstorms in South Devon at eleven in the morning.

❧ 4 ❧

1612 It was claimed that John Gregory of Stoke Gabriel had slandered his neighbour Mary Cowte by calling her a whore, 'bottle-arse jade' and 'burnt-arse jade'.

1653 Barnstaple's mayor tried to justify why only two seamen responded to his impressment notice.

1771 A woman threw herself from Exeter bridge to drown in the river.

1793 Mary Symons, the wife of a Plympton St Mary butcher, published in *The Exeter Gazette* her reasons for leaving her husband including that he beat her and forced her to have an abortion.

1800 Death at Iddesleigh of the Reverend William Tasker, author of 'An Ode to the Warlike Genius of Britain'.

1913 The National League for Opposing Women's Suffrage held a public meeting at Exmouth.

onions for seed. Make new plantations of strawberries if these were not made in July or August. Prune and tie raspberries, and make fresh plantations. In mild

FEBRUARY

❧ 5 ❧

1677 A Barnstaple vessel, with coal from Swansea, sank off the Welsh coast and all the crew and passengers drowned.

1792 A sermon on the slave trade was given at Ashburton.

1881 Fire caused serious damage to a basket factory in Devonport.

❧ 6 ❧

1584 Adrian Gilbert of Greenway near Dartmouth acquired a patent to search for the North West passage to China.

1772 Heavy snow caused accidents throughout Exeter.

1792 A public meeting on slavery in Ashburton argued that 'the traffic in the human species [was] being judged irreligious, inhuman and impolite'.

1824 Strawberries were on sale in the Exeter market.

1847 The setting of fires followed on from threatening letters in Colyton.

1880 A solar halo was seen at Babbacombe.

1882 Opening of the Devonport Free Library.

❧ 7 ❧

1792 The number of 'mad dogs' in Exeter caused the mayor to order all dogs to be cleared from the streets.

1793 A peach tree was in full blossom in Exmouth.

1876 A 'diamatie' licence was granted for the circus at Ellacombe, Torquay.

weather expose freely carnations and auriculas; plant also ranunculus roots. Prune such roses as are of robust growth. ✽ 1898 – *Sow beans and peas in the*

FEBRUARY

❧ 8 ❧

1587 Church bells were rung when the news reached Halberton that Mary Queen of Scots was executed.

1651 Five women from Payhembury were paid six pence a day for their four days' labour in planting beans.

1685 A thatcher in Cullompton received two shillings for three days' work (in addition to food and drink).

1882 Gluttony was decided as a Plymouth woman's cause of death who had collapsed on Bedford Street.

❧ 9 ❧

1822 More than 500 children in Plymouth had whooping cough.

1875 A Penny Reading was held in Germansweek.

1875 It was rumoured in Dartmouth that the *Britannia* would be replaced by a purpose-built Naval College.

❧ 10 ❧

1726 The Red Lion in Tiverton had a sale of silver plate.

1727 The snuff on sale in Exeter included Old Spanish, Best Brazil, Fine Old Seville, Fine Havana, The Right Gillicrankee, and Fine Myrtle Flavour.

1799 The *Weazle* set sail from Barnstaple and sunk at night in a storm with the loss of one woman and the crew of 105 men.

1819 The Devon & Exeter Institution allocated £200 for a Museum Room.

1824 A pair of Siamese twins, born in Kingsbridge, died and was exhibited in a museum belonging to a local doctor.

beginning and end of the month; a few early cabbages, red cabbages and savoys in the last week. Sow also early horn carrots, Dutch turnips, onions for a full

FEBRUARY

1829 The *Gleaner* sailed from Torquay for St John's, Newfoundland, with freight and emigrants.

1840 Queen Victoria wore a veil of Honiton lace at her wedding.

1900 At Sidmouth three volunteers for the South African War were given a farewell supper, silk handkerchief, testament and one pound of tobacco each.

❧ 11 ❧

1591 A Plymouth merchant was murdered by his wife and her lover.

1845 The *Louisa*, a schooner of 160 tons, was launched at Barnstaple.

1866 A heavy gale caused damage in East Devon.

1876 Kernick's Vegetable Worm Lozenges, 'No family would be without a box', were available for sale at Stone & Son, Exeter.

❧ 12 ❧

1849 An Australian emigrant ship was expected at Torquay.

1869 A flock of Egyptian Geese was seen near Exeter.

1889 An Exmouth woman, seen earlier leaving a public house with several naval reserve men, was convicted of using obscene language.

❧ 13 ❧

1638 Gilbert Staplehill of Dartmouth, former mayor, was buried with the following monument:
> *Behold thyself by me*
> *I was as thou art now*

crop in light soils, with a few leeks. Strawberries may be planted about the end of the month. Continue transplanting of hardy biannual flowers. On mild days

FEBRUARY

And thou in time shalt be
Even dust as I am now
So doth this figure paint to thee
The form and state of each degree.

1639   A gold sotter pot, porringer, spoon and fork were included amongst the plate at Tawstock Court near Barnstaple.

1823   Mr Thiodon's Original, Mechanical and Picturesque Theatre of Arts performed in Exeter featuring 'The Extraordinary and Unrivalled Automation Rope-Dancer'.

1879   Ladies and gentlemen at St George's Hall Ball in Plymouth were given their Valentines at midnight.

1881 (14th–15th)   Nearly three inches of rain fell in Ashburton.

❧ 14 ❦
St Valentine's Day

1628   Half an ounce of rhubarb bought at Forde House in Newton Abbot cost more at one shilling and six pence than either the 400 pilchards, 300 oysters, 3 pounds of soap or 2 rabbits.

1773   It was reported in Exeter that a female servant in Stonehouse found a gold ring in a turbot.

1822   The Plymouth Naval Club held a dinner in honour of the victory of Cape St Vincent.

1822   Around 700 Valentines were delivered in Exeter.

1835   A labourer of Holbeton was informed of his inheritance worth £30,000 in cash and extensive property in London.

1845   An inquest, held into the death of Elizabeth Bird, a woman of sixty who suddenly collapsed while coming out of a shop in Chulmleigh, decided she 'Died by the Visitation of God'.

1881   A great flood at Colyton.

admit air freely to auriculas, etc. ✸ *1900 – Sow early long pod beans. August-sown cabbages which were pricked out may now be planted. Plant onions for*

FEBRUARY

❧ 15 ❧

1765 A crowd gathered in Exeter to watch a bakery burn.

1835 A Holbeton labourer, who had just inherited several tens of thousands of pounds, maintained his daily duties with the explanation 'I had only heard it, but had not [yet] got it'.

1849 It was reported from Teignmouth that because of the improved weather 'umbrellas, clogs and gutta percha have given place to parasols and thinner boots and shoes, and a sort of getout stir-a-bout mania prevails'.

1943 *Bambi* played at the Exeter Savoy.

1978 (15th–19th) Four snowstorms swept through Devon with drifts over ten feet.

❧ 16 ❧

1287 Repairs were made to Walter, Exeter Cathedral Bell.

1645 The last battle of the Civil War took place at Torrington where the church was destroyed by an explosion and 'deforming many houses in the town, but killed some of the prisoners in the church, and some of our men that were in the church-yard'.

1770 One box of Kendrick's Worm Cakes from Mrs Mary Lee of Exeter cost a shilling.

1824 It was reported that more than 8,000 people, including servants, had dinner at Killerton House between 1st July 1823 and 1st January 1824.

1940 HMS *Exeter* returned to Plymouth after her battle with the *Graf Spee*.

seed. Sow peas the first favourable opportunity. Sow early radishes. Make new plantations of strawberries if not made in July or August. Plant edgings of

FEBRUARY

❧ 17 ❧

1604   Burial of Joan Gale, a widow who was described as 'a poor dark woman', at Salcombe.

1863   A male 'clouded saffron' butterfly was captured in a Broadwoodkelly garden.

1881   The Plymouth Workhouse had a musical entertainment.

❧ 18 ❧

1629   Richard Lewis' punishment for fathering Joan Waterman's illegitimate baby was to pay fifteen pence weekly maintenance whereas she was publicly whipped.

1663   Strong winds prompted one Barnstaple writer to claim that 'the like was never heard here with us in England'.

1726   The Knave of Clubs, a brick house in St Leonards with a yard suitable for tennis, was for sale.

1772   An infant was found dissected into pieces in an earthen jar in Exeter.

1876   The first words misspelled at a spelling bee held at the Beacon Assembly Rooms in Exmouth were kiln, height, hearse and scythe.

1882   *Dick Whittington and his Cat* played its last performance in Plymouth.

❧ 19 ❧

1657   Death at Topsham of 'old John Padden' who reputedly was 111 years old.

1799   A shipwrecked sailor was buried at Mortehoe.

1901   Teignmouth lumpers were reportedly unhappy at the lack of work.

various kinds, such as box, thrift, daisies and London pride. Plant ranunculus roots in mild weather, in rich loamy soil. Prune Chinese roses. ✽ *1901 – Sow*

FEBRUARY

❧ 20 ❧

Astrological Sign of PISCES, the Fishes
(through to March 20th)

1547 At Plymouth there was a 'triumph' (a public pageant) to mark the coronation of Edward VI.

1793 Thomas Payne's effigy was hanged on a gibbet in the Valley of Rocks and burned.

1833 The county's elms particularly suffered in a storm which hit in the morning.

1877 A 100 yard race was conducted in Wonford for the wager of a dozen eggs.

1915 An editorial in *The Exeter Flying Post* lamented the reluctance of farmers' sons to enlist for war service.

❧ 21 ❧

1643 Roger Boaman was overheard in Parliamentarian-held Exeter saying 'God Bless the King and hang the Parliament'.

1829 Exeter constables searched for those responsible for the obscene language written in chalk on window shutters.

1861 A hurricane hit in the morning causing the county wide-spread damage.

❧ 22 ❧

1849 It was reported that Roman vases and an Elizabethan coin were found during digging at the New Inn in Exeter.

1876 John Bryant, 17, was charged with stealing a beer glass from the Elephant Inn in Exeter.

1879 The last performance of *Jack and the Bean Stalk* at Plymouth.

peas, the first favourable opportunity. Sow early long-pod beans for a main crop, and early radishes in a dry and sheltered situation. Plant onions for seed.

FEBRUARY

❧ 23 ❧

1792   Death of Sir Joshua Reynolds: it was written his portraits 'remind the spectator of the invention of history and the amenity of landscape'.

1823   One of the turrets of Shaugh Prior church was destroyed by lightning.

1829   Bengal tigers, alpacas, lions, zebras, leopards, pumas, porcupines, an ostrich, pelicans and an elephant were on show as Atkins' Royal Menagerie at Exeter.

1843   Two men stole 3 Golden pheasants from Pince's nursery in St Thomas.

1866   Dick Tom Upton of Tiverton was committed to six weeks' imprisonment for stealing a silk umbrella.

1916 (23rd–26th)   Heavy snow fell at Princetown causing drifts up to ten feet high.

❧ 24 ❧

1664   Baptism of Thomas Newcomen, inventor of the steam engine, at Dartmouth.

1824   Mr Ronchetti exhibited at Exeter his museum of 'natural and artificial curiosities consisting of birds, beasts, fishes, reptiles, works of art and wonderful productions of nature' which cost ladies and gentlemen one shilling and tradespeople and children only six pence.

1881   A Devonport team won £15 in a game of billiards.

Make new plantations of strawberries if these were not made in July or August. Prune and tie raspberries, and make fresh plantations. In mild weather expose

FEBRUARY

❧ 25 ❧

1629　Lenten provisions at Forde House in Newton Abbot included herring, cockles, lobsters, oysters and dried codfish.

1785　Lily of the Valley, violets and minionet were in flower in the Grape House at Saltram.

1822　*Othello* was performed at Exeter.

1904　The first woman to take out a driving license in Exeter was Miss Katherine Rose Budd.

1929 (25th–26th)　A 'glazed' frost broke telephone wires and pulled down trees.

❧ 26 ❧

1821　Fire destroyed the Red Lion Inn in Honiton.

1848　An innkeeper in Paris Street in Exeter was fined for keeping pigs and claimed he was unaware that the law differed from his native Tiverton where pigs were allowed.

1866　A 'German Tree' was placed in the centre of Holsworthy Market Hall as part of a fundraising effort.

❧ 27 ❧

1665　Francis Edgcumbe and John Skelton fought a duel to the death at Plymouth.

1799　A shipwrecked sailor was buried at Mortehoe.

1915　Five men in the Devon Regiment were reported to have been killed in battle or died from their wounds in the past week.

freely carnations and auriculas; plant also ranunculus roots. Prune such roses as are of robust growth. ❋ *1907 – Prepare all the ground intended for early*

FEBRUARY

❧ 28 ❧

1619   A survey of mariners in south Devon revealed there were 3,653 seamen resident on the county's south coast.

1741   Mr Beere of Honiton sold Dr Daffy's Famous Cordial Elixir.

1793   Dr Waite's 'celebrated Worm Medicine in the form of ginger nuts' was available from T.K. Sweeting, Newton-Bushel druggist.

1823   Apricot trees bloomed in a gentleman's garden in Teignmouth.

1883   It was lamented in *The Exeter Flying Post* that 'everything seems now to be managed the same way. Agitate, agitate, agitate, or you will not get what you want'.

❧ 29 ❧
Leap Day

1620   Alexander Cary was convicted of being a masterless vagrant and ordered to be whipped and returned home to Plymouth

1848   It was reported that Henry Ellis, Exeter silversmith, had 'very beautiful specimens of articles of ornament and utility' from silver extracted from the Combe Martin silver mine which had been purchased by, among others, the Queen.

1881   A breakfast banquet was held in Plymouth for soldiers.

crops. When the weather is suitable continue sowing every fortnight peas, beans, onions, lettuces, savoys, celery, spinach, cauliflowers, carrots and parsnips. ✳ ✳ ✳

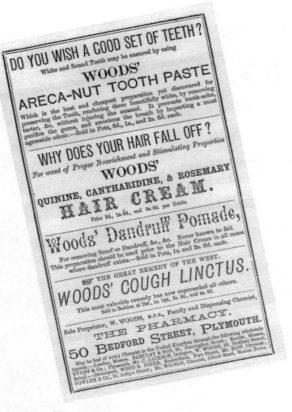
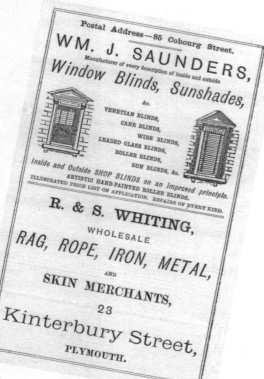

MARCH

March dust to be sold,
Worth ransoms of gold.

Thomas Tusser, 1557

MARCH

❧ 1 ❧

1160   The nuns of Polsloe were granted a burial ground.

1651   Thomas Larkham, vicar of Tavistock, was given several raspberry pies by a parishioner.

1847   A company of comedians performed in Dartmouth.

1899   A report to the Bideford Rural District Sanitary Authority noted one case of scarlet fever in Abbotsham and one of puerperal fever in Clovelly.

❧ 2 ❧

Birthday of Sir Thomas Bodley, founder of the Oxford library: born at Exeter, 1545.

1615   Orders were given in Exeter that any person 'posed, barbed or trimmed' on a Sunday should be fined three shillings and four pence.

1829   A report from Barnstaple claimed that a turnip measuring 5 feet and 1½ inches long was dug up.

❧ 3 ❧

1606   William Zevie, the 'deaf and dumb' servant of William Towill, was buried at Stokeinteignhead.

1606   Baptism of William Davenant, author of *Newes from Plimouth* in which a character claims 'this town is dearer than Jerusalem after a year's siege, they would make us pay for daylight if they knew how to measure the sun beams by the yard. Nay, sell the very air too if they could serve it out in fine China

❋❋❋ 1891 – *The main crops of vegetables should be put in the ground. Strike calceolarias, verbenas, scarlet geraniums, fuchsias, Chinese chrysanthemums*

MARCH

bottles. If you walk but 3 turns in the H igh Street they will ask you money for wearing out the pebbles'.

1631   Dartmouth's mayor assured the government there was sufficient grain locally despite the national shortage and pleaded for the town's ale houses to remain open because of the high number of visiting sailors.

1895   Snow fell in Exmouth.

1990   In Plymouth a demonstration was held against the Poll Tax.

❧ 4 ❧

1636   Alice Tanner of Heavitree allegedly slandered Alice Bartlett by calling her a whore, errant whore, common whore and a 'hackney' whore.

1823   An Exeter tradesman spent an evening with Sir John Barley-corn in the Jolly Knight [sic] and instead of walking home found himself waking up in Tiverton the following morning.

1839   Edmund Kean performed in *Macbeth* in Exeter.

1880   Plymouth's mayor gave £1 2s 6d to the Lifeboat crew for saving the *Hankow*, an Australian steamship, in the recent storm.

❧ 5 ❧

1593   A silver whistle was one of the most valuable items owned by Gilbert Peron of Littleham at the time of his death.

1764   A new service, the 'Machine', started from Exeter offering transport to London in two days.

&c. Plant gladioluses. This month is the best time for grafting fruit-trees.
✳ *1896 – Sow peas for succession. The first favourable weather, transplant in*

MARCH

1824 The Stover Fox Hounds ran a fox fourteen miles for one hour and twenty minutes before catching 'old Hector' within a mile of Teignmouth.

1832 It was reported that a rat weighing 3lb 5oz was caught near Barnstaple.

❧ 6 ❧

1823 The temporary ceiling of the Unitarian Church in Exeter, erected 'to lessen the vocal exertion of Dr Carpenter', fell down.

1843 A bullock ran amok through the streets of Totnes.

1852 Emigrants were able to book passage from Plymouth on the *John* to New York and on the *Queen Victoria* to Quebec.

1871 A strong wind blew through Ashburton.

1942 The Minister for Agriculture opened a Hostel for Land Girls in Moretonhampstead.

❧ 7 ❧

1820 Fire destroyed Exeter's theatre.

1845 Sarah Ellen Harris, a 'begging impostor and itinerant preacher', was sent to prison at Bideford for selling tracts without a licence.

1902 King Edward VII laid the foundation stone of the Royal Naval College at Dartmouth.

1930 A public meeting debated whether the county council or the police should pay the estimated £9,000 needed to run electric traffic lights in Devon.

rows across a warm border the beans from the autumn-sown beds. Sow cabbage on a warm border during the first or second week for summer or autumn supply.

MARCH

❧ 8 ❧

1824   Two brothers, aged 10 and 12 years old, were accused of being part of a 'gang of juvenile depredators' in Exeter.

1845   G.R. Ball, Perruquier and Hair Cutter, of the Strand in Torquay, offered for sale Delcroix & Company's celebrated *Poudre Subtile* which removed the Greatest Blemish to the beauty of women (superfluous hair on the face, neck and arms) in less than ten minutes without pain or injury to the skin.

1871   Snow fell on Dartmoor.

1895   Primroses were picked in Broadhempston.

1922   Winds reached 96 mph in Plymouth.

1930   A letter to the editor of *The Devon & Exeter Gazette* derided the amount of money spent on promoting tourism in Devon.

❧ 9 ❧

1639   An Irish harp, a violin, a viol, an organ with virginal, and a double bass viol were located in the staircase of Tawstock Court .

1824   The editor of *The Western Luminary* informed his readers of the establishment in London of the 'National Institution for the Preservation of Life from Shipwreck'.

1829   The 'Lowreyian Bonnet', invented by Mrs Lowrey of Exeter, went on sale for summer wear.

1863   Nine persons died in an explosion in a pyrotechnic's shop in Plymouth as the owner prepared fireworks for the forthcoming marriage of the Prince of Wales.

1891 (9th–10th)   A blizzard hit the West Country.

1895   A large elm tree, said to be over 200 years old, was felled in Uffculme.

Sow broad-leaved London leeks and lettuce. Make new plantings of mint. Sow onions. Sow parsley. Sow a few of the hardiest annuals about the end of the

MARCH

❧ 10 ❧

1634 Thomas Halswell was ordered to maintain a footpath through a close known as South Ridge in Stoke Fleming and erect 'sufficient and easy stiles in their ancient places'.

1828 Small pox was prevalent in Torrington.

1832 A 'tide of emigration to the United States' was said to have swept through Barnstaple, Bideford, Exeter and Thorverton.

1923 The London Bidefordian Society held a Whist Drive at the Strand in London.

❧ 11 ❧

1828 The Edinburgh Steam Carriage was on show in Exeter.

1832 It was reported that five men were taken from the county gaol to Devonport where they were to be transported overseas.

1845 Heavy snow fell throughout Devon and it made Tiverton look 'more white and picturesque than ever'.

❧ 12 ❧

1659 Philip Bartlett overheard a neighbour say that Exeter's clergy were thieves, robbers, 'mere deluders of the people' and 'ravening' wolves in sheep's clothing.

1789 The recovery of George III was marked in Exeter with illuminations and among the mottoes were 'Long Live the King', 'May the Happiness of Britian be extended to the world', 'He Lives', 'Thanks be to Him, who has given us cause for this', and, over an apothecary's shop, 'God save the King – success to physic'.

month; thin out some of those sown in autumn. ❋ 1898 – *Sow main crops of peas, beans, cabbages, onions, leeks, carrots, parsnips, Brussels sprouts, borecoles,*

MARCH

1800 A Newton Bushel potato farmer was thrown into a fire for telling the poor that they should eat bramble leaves if they could not afford food.

1823 Flags were paraded and an effigy burnt in Bideford regarding a disputed tax for the poor.

1832 Two emigrant ships destined for the United States lay at anchor at Teignmouth.

1845 Wombwell's Menagerie of Beasts and Birds continued on show at Exeter.

1889 Tiverton was unable to field a team against Exeter and lost 1 – 0 in what was described as 'the shortest time on record' in football.

❧ 13 ❧

Birthday of John Bidgood, Exeter physician: born at Exeter, 1623

1285 The Bishop agreed that two Exeter churches, Saint Paul and Saint Cuthbert, were to be joined.

1832 A trout weighing 23½ pounds, and measuring two feet and ten inches long, was caught in the river Clyst near Topsham.

1876 An eight-year old boy shot a Snowy Owl at Ditsworthy Warren near Plymouth.

1900 At Torquay Police Court Samuel Waymouth was fined 18s for working a horse in an unfit condition, George Vyvian was fined 6s 6d for riding a bicycle on the pleasure grounds at Babbacombe and Frederick Harold Westcott was imprisoned for a fortnight for not maintaining his wife.

lettuces and spinach. In the beginning and also at the end of the month sow turnips and savoys. In the last fortnight sow asparagus, cauliflowers, celery,

MARCH

❧ 14 ❦

1755 Impressment caused a shortage of workmen in Lympstone.

1768 Three soldiers were arrested for raping a woman on the road from Crediton to Sandford.

1770 After a performance of *King Henry the Fifth* in Exeter there was 'an entire dance of cows, goats and sheep'.

1845 Friends brought 107 ploughs and ploughed 84 acres as a token of respect to Mr Reynolds of Raddon Court in Thorverton.

1871 Snow fell on Ashburton at night.

1895 The anthrax outbreak in Ilfracombe continued.

1900 The Devon and Exeter Gardener's Association heard a lecture by Mr T. Slade, gardener to Lord Poltimore, on 'The Treatment of Amaryllis'.

❧ 15 ❦
Ides of March

1717 The *Concord* of Topsham, bound for New England, was forced by contrary winds into Dartmouth.

1823 It was reported that a lady's maid employed for five weeks at Kingsbridge was discovered to be a male impostor.

1866 A gale swept through Devon.

1900 A concert given at the Exeter Workingmen's Society's Market Hall was well-attended and it was reported that 'a very pretty skirt dance was executed by Miss Winnie Cole'.

&c. Plant the main crop of potatoes during the last fortnight. Sow hardy annuals about the end of the month. ❀ *1900 – Transplant autumn-sown beans the first*

MARCH

❧ 16 ❦

1767 Fire broke out in Ottery St Mary at ten in the morning.

1789 The recovery of George III was marked at Ottery St Mary by church bells, roasting an ox, drinking four hogsheads of cider, a band playing 'God Save the King', and bonfires and illuminations.

1832 Three adders were found and killed on a hedge in Fremington.

1854 In Barnstaple a reward of fifty pounds was offered for the identity of the author of *The Scourge*.

1882 Miss Helen Blackburn gave a lecture on 'The rise and progress of the women's suffrage movement' at the Borough Arms Coffee House in Plymouth.

❧ 17 ❦

1623 Two Stokeinteignhead mariners bound for Newfoundland were attacked by pirates.

1628 Lady Lucy Reynell of Forde House in Newton Abbot purchased one ounce of rhubarb for three shillings and six pence.

1675 Punishments were fixed for two women found guilty of poisoning Elizabeth Weeks & her mother of Plymouth: Phillipa Carey was to be hanged and Anne Evans burned.

1899 The admission for hearing a lecture on 'Manures & Feeding Stuffs' at Hartland was one penny.

favourable weather. Sow early purple sprouting and dwarf late broccoli in the last week of the month. Sow cabbage for summer and autumn supply. Sow a few

MARCH

❧ 18 ❦

1555 Burial at Bovey Tracey of Thomas Libyett who had been murdered, his body placed in a furse brake and then eaten to the bone by pigs.

1588 John Anthony, 'a neyger', was buried at Plymouth

1629 Lady Lucy Reynell of Forde House in Newton Abbot purchased 400 oysters for sixteen pence.

❧ 19 ❦

1767 A woman and child were unharmed by their house collapsing during high winds in Exeter.

1770 Old Barebones beat Blind Jenny in a one half mile heat at Berry Down near Barnstaple.

1793 It was reported from Plymouth that the Channel was 'swarming' with French privateers.

1845 The 'Devonshire Giant Ox', raised in Bridestowe and claimed to weigh over 3,700 pounds, was exhibited in Exeter.

1869 A gale blew down an elm tree in Northam and sunk several barges in the river Torridge.

1889 It was reported that an inquest was held into the death of an Exeter infant who had lived on a diet of condensed milk.

❧ 20 ❦

1830 It was reported from Exeter that 'among the numerous individuals whom bustle, business and botheration called into activity during the Assize, none was more like to obtain that portion of celebrity which fall to the share of every well-

early horn carrots in a warm situation for use before the main crop is ready. Sow leeks. Make new plantations of mint. Sow onions about the middle of the month.

MARCH

intentioned man than Mr William Washington, an American gentleman.' Washington, who 'comes from the land of liberty' and was employed in selling soap for eradicating stains, was accused of taking the liberty of stealing another man's jacket.

1852 The Display of New Spring Shawls continued at Green & Bennets, Exeter.

1882 Margaret Waterfield, an elderly nurse, slipped in Exeter on an orange peel and later died from 'exhaustion and shock to the system'.

1914 A blizzard brought fifteen inches of snow to Princetown.

1930 The county's coldest day of the year was recorded at Tavistock at 19°.

1941 At around nine o'clock the Luftwaffe began to systematically destroy Plymouth. Over the next few months thousands of buildings were destroyed and many hundreds killed.

❧ 21 ❧
Astrological Sign of ARIES, the Ram
(through to April 20th)

1620 Rabice Shepeyard of Black Torrignton admitted to stealing a gander, 2 roasting pigs, 2 ducks and 9 goose eggs.

1727 A concert of vocal and instrumental music was given at the music room near St Catherine's Gate in Exeter.

1829 A critic described Fanny Ayton as having a powerful voice and being a 'very interesting' actress in *The Prima Donna* at the King's Theatre in Plymouth.

1839 Nell Gwynne beat seven horses in the Teignbridge Steeple Chase.

Sow parsley. ❀ *1901 – Sow peas for succession. The first favourable weather, transplant in rows across a warm border the beans from the autumn-sown beds.*

MARCH

1845 Hot Cross Buns were in heavy demand in Exeter.

1857 Members of the Exeter Literary Society heard a lecture on 'The Romance of the Law Courts'.

1942 (21st–28th) Exeter's Warship Week

22

1830 *Woolmer's Exeter and Plymouth Gazette* reported that a 'stupid-looking, half-witted farmer, scarcely acquainted with his own name' had accused another man of stealing his watch while drinking to excess in St Sidwell's parish, Exeter.

1845 A party of Sappers and Miners was surveyed a new map in Ivybridge.

1845 It was reported in *Woolmer's Exeter and Plymouth Gazette* that a proposition had been made to alter all clocks in England to agree with the Greenwich meridian.

1847 Railway whistles, a new invention, were on sale in Exeter.

23

1610 Pirates, led by Thomas Salkeld, captured Lundy Island and declared him King.

1852 A lecture was given at the Colyton Mutual Improvement Society on 'The Properties of Matter' which was said to have been 'such an intellectual treat the inhabitants have rarely had an opportunity of being present at'.

1857 The Halsdon Hounds met at Glen Cottage, the Eggesford Hounds met at Stone Moor and the Tiverton Fox Hounds at Oakford Bridge.

Sow cabbage on a warm border during the first or second week for summer or autumn supply. Sow broad-leaved London leeks and lettuce. Make new plantings

MARCH

❧ 24 ❧

1190 Richard I granted Exeter's burgesses freedom from paying tolls in fairs and markets.

1605 The Halberton and Totnes church bells were rung to mark the accession of James I two years earlier.

1788 At Heavitree three smugglers were hanged for murder.

1845 A yellow butterfly was seen flying near Exeter.

1875 Members of the Royal North Devon Golf Club engaged in the 'manly exercise' at the Easter Meeting.

1978 The National Trust opened Killerton House to the public.

2000 The Mayor of Exeter was given the first copy of *The Devon Almanac* at the Guildhall.

❧ 25 ❧

Quarter Day / Lady Day
(Annunciation of Blessed Virgin Mary)

1588 'Raleigh', a native of North America, was baptised in Bideford.

1651 John Willoughby of Payhembury paid a Honiton tinker to mend kettles and a warming pan.

1829 One of the largest foxhunts known in Devon took place at Cowley Bridge with 250 riders, 'some 40 or 50 in scarlet', and another 150 on foot.

1936 At Buckfast Abbey the Lord Abbot blessed a new bell, weighing 7½ tons and named Hosanna.

of mint. Sow onions. Sow parsley. Sow a few of the hardiest annuals about the end of the month; thin out some of those sown in autumn. ❋ 1907 – *The main*

MARCH

❧ 26 ❧

Birthday of Agnes Weston, organizer of the Sailors' Rests: born at London, 1840.

1595 Richard Champernowne of Modbury denied a rumour that he was 'a gelder of boys for preserving their voices'.

1676 St Thomas had a great number of small pox deaths.

1789 Two sheep and an ox were roasted in Moretonhampstead to mark the recovery of George III.

1852 Mr D. Mackintosh delivered, to a full audience at the Modbury Institution, a lecture on 'Ethnograpy' which was 'a classification of the inhabitants of England according to the physical and mental characteristics of the various Celtic and Teutonic tribes from which they are descended, illustrated by dressed and stuffed male and female models'.

1875 A Torrington engine failed to put out a fire in a South Street grocery but fortunately the Bideford engine, which had been sent a telegram, was able to help.

❧ 27 ❧

1610 The *Elizabeth* of Dover brought in a cargo of malt and hops to Topsham.

1643 William Browne, Tavistock poet, was buried.

1800 It was reported that Barnstaple's mayor had converted his house into a 'soup shop' for the poor.

1914 The St Thomas Rural Council discussed public concerns of infection from the city's consumptive sanatorium and complaints that patients had visited shops in Pinhoe as well as the Post Office.

crops of vegetables should be put in the ground during this month. Sow asparagus, Brussels sprouts, cauliflower, celery, broccoli, spinach, beets, onions, peas and

MARCH

❧ 28 ❧

1663 It was reported that *The Cheats*, a new comedy by John Wilson of Plymouth, 'has been attempted on the stage but is so scandalous that it was forbidden'.

1675 Burial of a widow, her daughter and grand-daughter in a single grave at Topsham.

1879 Six months' imprisonment was given to a naval deserter at Plymouth who pleaded seasickness as his excuse.

❧ 29 ❧

1831 Among the approved medicines sold by Longman of Sidmouth were Ching's Worm Lozenges, Fothergill's Nervous Drops and Butler's Pectoral Elixir.

1836 A storm hit the county with heavy wind, snow, hail and rain.

1942 Jean Arthur featured in *The Devil & Miss Jones* at the Exeter Plaza.

❧ 30 ❧

1764 Exeter's theatre offered a concert and a performance of *King Richard III*.

1770 A drink composed of herbs, roots, plants and bark, was available as 'English Coffee' from W. Grigg of Exeter.

1833 Dr Barnard sold in his Cathedral Yard shop Dr Swedanberg's Vegetable Pills which were 'so famous through Germany, Prussia, Poland and the Continent of Europe for more than a century' in treating venereal disease.

beans, parsnips, turnips, and rooted radishes. Plant red cabbage, kidney beans, seakale and cauliflowers from frames, and sow melons and cucumbers in hot

MARCH

1835   Charles Macready played Macbeth at Exeter.

1852   A donation of twenty pounds was made towards the construction of the Exeter Baths and Wash-houses.

❧ 31 ❧

1717   The *Dove Hoy* of Dartmouth, laden with a cargo of stones, was stranded at Slapton Sands.

1823   Bull baiting took place at St Thomas.

1835   Charles Macready played in *William Tell* at Exeter.

1970   Diana Rigg's nude scene helped ticket sales for the opening night of *Abelard and Heloise* at the Northcott Theatre in Exeter.

beds. Dress borders and strawberry beds, and finish pruning. Strike calceolarias, verbenas, scarlet geraniums, fuchsias, Chinese chrysanthemums &c. ✻✻✻

APRIL

Well-apparell'd April on the heels of limping winter treads

William Shakespeare,
Romeo and Juliet,
Act I, Scene 2

APRIL

❧ 1 ⚶

1598 At Exeter a woman was whipped for having three illegitimate children.

1620 Leonard Trickey, a Culmstock husbandman, denied taking six pounds of his master's tallow with felonious intent and claimed the tallow he hid in his trousers was done merely to see whether it would be missed.

1704 The parishioners of Great Nerkworthy held a fete to honour the king's coronation.

1770 Two 'footpads' robbed John Pike of Venn Ottery of a gold guinea and four shillings.

1835 Charles Macready played Hamlet at Exeter.

1845 Hounds killed three otters at Peamore.

1889 The first meeting of the County Council was held.

1920 The Lundy postmaster left the island for his first break in 24 years.

❧ 2 ⚶

1676 Twenty-eight shillings and seven pence were collected at Topsham for ransoming three Dartmouth residents taken by Barbary pirates.

1845 Lord Sidmouth's new house at Upottery, built by the architect Samuel A. Greig, was nearly completed.

1852 The Slapton Hounds met at Pollard's Sands Hotel and William Bastard was presented with a silver hunting horn as a token of the Hunt's esteem.

❀❀❀ 1891 – *Sow whatever was omitted last month. Continue the sowing of asparagus, brocoli, Dutch turnips, &c. Plant out rhubarb, seakale, artichokes,*

APRIL

❧ 3 ❧

1598 In the early afternoon fire swept through Tiverton and several hundred houses were destroyed within a few hours. It was said 'the rich men of the town were unmerciful to the poor and suffered them to die in the streets for want'.

1620 Jane Adams of Ide claimed she allowed William West to have the 'carnal knowledge of her body' on a promise of marriage.

1789 A loose knot was responsible for a man at Heavitree falling to the ground before it was retied and the man successfully executed.

1817 Princess Cariboo of Javasu (aka Mary Wilcocks of Witheridge) appeared in Gloucestershire.

1861 It was reported that a group of working men at Exeter considered forming a cooperative society.

❧ 4 ❧

1442 The Mayor of Dartmouth was ordered to arrest Alice Mulner of Dartmouth in connection with the theft of 14 tuns of white wine.

1581 Francis Drake was knighted by Elizabeth I on the *Golden Hind* which was maintained at Deptford as a national memorial.

1835 The road from Bridgerule was reportedly 'literally crowded with families leaving their native lands for the wilds of America'.

1842 Alexander Pontey advertised his Plymouth Nursery offering 23 varieties of Pelargoniums including Jupiter, Wildfire and Lifeguardsman.

1905 The electric tramway was opened in Exeter.

and small salading. Earth up peas; tie up lettuces. Finish the grafting of fruit-trees. Sow annuals, biennals, and perennials. Plant evergreens; propagate by

APRIL

5

1765 A pair of Newfoundland dogs recently brought to Lympstone were said to be too ferocious to be allowed near the public.

1826 An auction was held in Plymouth of 'the whole of a magnificent plateau of the most exquisite sculpture, in Florentine alabaster, consisting of statues, temples, figures, monumental trophies' which had been ordered by Josephine Bonaparte in 1810.

1882 Plymouth workingmen held a mass meeting regarding the foreign sugar bounty system but it ended in 'divided opinion and confusion'.

1940 Readers of *The Western Times* were encouraged to 'Plough the fields, increase their yields. Plough up your grassland. Make every field give a greater yield. You cannot grow guns and 'planes; but you can grow more food and more root and fodder crops, so releasing ships to carry guns and 'planes. Make no mistake – ploughing is the key to victory – and the key is in your hands'.

6

Birthday of Philip Henry Gosse, zoologist: born at Worcester, 1810.

1294 A lease was renewed on a Totnes house for the annual rent of six shillings.

1596 Burial of Grace, the 'neiger servant' of a Barnstaple merchant and one of the earliest Africans recorded in Devon.

1845 Two thatched cottages in Hockworthy burned to the ground.

1864 A cuckoo was heard near Exeter.

cutting all the woody kitchen shrubs. ✱ *1896 – In the first fortnight plant the second early crop of potatoes, and the main crop about the end of the month. Sow*

APRIL

1880　**O**nly five days after April 1 Sir Harry Bottle Brush, Sir Thomas Bacon Fat and Sir Blinkum Blakum acted as Starters for Ilfracombe's *Grand International Steeple Chaise*.

∂ **7** ∽

1606　**I**t was claimed that this was 'as fair a day for the weather as hath been known at such time of the year this many years'.

1823　*The Pretender*, a new play recently translated, was performed in Exeter but the critic noted that Mr Frimbley would not give over his 'monkey tricks' and that in general 'the double allusions seemed too broad to be witty and too coarse to meet the ear of decency'.

1829　**G**eorge Spreat of Paignton advertised in a local newspaper that he was no longer financially responsible for bills in his wife's name she since 'eloped' from him.

1852　**A** young woman was arrested in Exeter for stealing a dress and parasol from Mrs Hurst's Temperance Lodging House.

∂ **8** ∽

1629　**L**ady Lucy Reynell of Forde House in Newton Abbot purchased beef, tongue, tripe and 'cows heels'.

1659　**T**he Reverend Thomas Larkham planted apricots at Tavistock.

1812　**T**wo French prisoners of war at Dartmoor Prison fought with daggers and died of their wounds.

1944　*The Devon & Exeter Gazette* asked that every man, woman and child be 'rat-reporters' in order to locate and destroy the 'food-devouring, disease-spreading pests'.

beans for succession. Sow red beetroot in the second week. About the same time sow borecole or Scotch greens and Brussels sprouts. Sow lettuce for succession

APRIL

❧ 9 ❦

Birthday of John Cook, Exeter notable: born at Ashburton, 1765.

1811 An Osprey was seen hunting for fish on the river Avon near Aveton Gifford Bridge.

1823 A public meeting held at the Plymouth Guildhall called for the abolition of slavery.

1832 A vessel anchored off Seaton with 205 emigrants for the United States.

❧ 10 ❦

1823 A benefit concert was held at the Exeter theatre. A reviewer noted that Miss Nightingale of Plymouth had the 'merit of singing in tune but her voice wants power for public display' and that Mr Spencer Kemp should not appear in public as a harper.

1830 It was reported from Exeter that Hyamm Isaacs, a 'converted Jew', preached to crowded congregations in the West Country.

1836 There was no music in Cullompton parish church because the organist received less than £7 for his previous year's wages.

1880 The new French fog bell began service at Plymouth Break-water.

1889 The events at the annual athletic sports day for the cadets of HMS *Britannia* were the long jump, quarter mile race, wheelbarrow race, 100 yards, throwing of a cricket ball, one mile race, three-legged race, hurdles and half-mile handicap.

once a month. Plant in a shady place slips of sage, thyme, rue and other herbs. In the fruit garden proceed with grafting. Make the main sowing of hardy

APRIL

❧ 11 ❧

1681 Edmund Tremayne of Collacombe paid eighteen shillings to Harry for shoeing horses.

1740 A Tiverton cloth-maker valued his property for insurance purposes as being worth £6,100.

1852 The cash box of the Sisters of Mercy was returned to the Plymouth Police Station.

1871 At Holne 2.25 inches of rain fell.

1885 The oldest Virgin in Devon was buried: Anne Virgin, aged 100, was interred in Membury.

1889 M. Mortimer won the Long Jump in the Teignmouth Grammar School annual sports day (12 feet, 7 inches).

❧ 12 ❧

1789 Death of Mr N. Jacobson of Plymouth, confectioner, and 'supposed to be the largest man in the West and though remarkably fat was able to walk to church within a week of his death'.

1852 The Temperance Festival in Exeter featured the Exeter Band of Hope.

1892 Beatrix Potter visited Exeter and wrote of it she was very fond.

1930 Harringcourt was the first Devon garden of the season to be opened to raise funds for the Queen Victoria Jubilee Institute and the Devonshire Nursing Association.

annuals this month. ❈ 1898 – *Sow asparagus, seakale, beet, carrots and onions on heavy soils. Sow broccoli and kidney beans both in the second and in the last*

APRIL

❧ 13 ❧

1647 In Exeter a public day of thanksgiving for the city's surrender from 'the enemies to the power of Parliament'.

1829 A mechanical chimney-sweeper was exhibited at Exeter which, it was claimed, would 'entirely do away with the necessity of employing boys'.

1841 It was reported that Joseph Clarke of Wolborough was sentenced to three weeks' imprisonment for stealing eggs.

1886 A Hoopoe was shot near Loddiswell.

❧ 14 ❧

1470 Edward IV began a visit to Exeter.

1829 Rumours circulated in Exeter that criminals were lurking to kidnap people and sell their corpses and it was suggested that children should be kept within doors at dark and not walk in deserted places.

1853 It was announced in the *Exeter Flying Post* that it was now possible to travel by rail from Exeter to Edinburgh on the same day.

1930 The public was enticed to go to the Palladium in Exeter for *The Hollywood Revue* with 'SEE and HEAR an allstar cast of 25 stars in the Screen's First Musical Revue'.

❧ 15 ❧

Birthday of William Gifford, satirist: born at Ashburton, 1756

1620 Those at Christow attending the funeral of Gilbert Davies,

week. Attend to the hoeing and thinning of the spinach, onions, turnips and stake up peas. Sow main or succession crops and annuals of all sorts. Biennials

APRIL

one of nineteen children, heard he was the 'fruit of a virtuous gentlewoman's womb, who was as a fruitful vine upon the walls of her husband's house'.

1717   A man from Dean Prior struck a neighbour on the forehead, from which he died, for claiming to have 'debauched' his daughter.

1822   Elizabeth Carter was transported overseas for stealing seven spoons from The Hotel [now The Clarence] in Exeter.

1825   The North Devon Friendly Institution was established for males and females between the ages of 10 and 50 of good character and sound health.

☙ 16 ❧

1607   It was rumoured that at Salcombe several hundred sailors were stealing boats, threatening to burn the town, committing murder and burying their victims in the sands.

1703   Captains Richard Kirby and Cooper Wade were brought to Plymouth on HMS *Bristol* and shot for cowardice and misconduct.

1810   The first turf was cut on the Great Western Canal at Holcombe Rogus.

1832   It was reported that an eagle, weighing ten pounds and with a wingspan of fourteen feet, was shot near Kingsbridge.

☙ 17 ❧

1824   It was debated in Exeter whether the cowslip was native to Devon.

and perennials should be sown before the middle of the month. Finish the transplanting of herbaceous plants by the end of the first week. ✻ *1900 – Sow*

APRIL

1826 A petition against slavery circulated through Barnstaple.

1835 A flock of martins were seen flying over a fishpond in Yealmpton.

1871 The aurora borealis was seen at Ashburton.

1876 The Easter Monday excursion from Ottery St Mary to Exmouth's baby show was the talk of the town as several parties lost their way at night and only reached home the following morning.

1900 An 'Engish Viper', presumably an adder, was caught and exhibited in Hartland.

1942 Clyst Hydon school children collected 510 eggs for the Royal Devon & Exeter Hospital Egg Week.

❧ 18 ❦

1601 John Davis set sail from Dartmouth for Malaysia on the first voyage of the East India Company.

1665 William Martyn of Ebford reported seeing 'strange apparitions in the air but I dare not traffic in such news lest I be reckoned among the fanatics and the fabulous authors'.

1770 Exeter celebrated the release of John Wilkes, politician, with the ringing of bells and by strangers and carriages being marked with the number 45.

1826 The *Devonshire Sporting Magazine* was proposed.

1876 Among the hack horses and colts sold by auction at Poltimore were Fanny, Brunette, Rob Roy, The Duke and Duchess, Nimrod and The Rubber.

beans for succession. Sow red beet in the first or second week. Sow Brussels sprouts about the second week. Sow the main crop of celery. If the main crop of

APRIL

❧ 19 ❧

Birthday of Sir Edward Pellew, Viscount Exmouth: born at Dover, 1757.

1629 Elizabeth Lovett allegedly called another Dartmouth woman a 'whore' and said she 'didest play the whore under a bay bush'.

1651 At Ottery St Mary 'Jane Hollard commonly called deaf Jane' was buried.

1717 It was reported that a Blackawton tailor, who weighed between three and four hundred weight (up to 448 pounds) and accounted 'a wonder of the age being one of the biggest men that ever was seen in these parts', claimed the Devil incited him in beating his wife to death.

1727 Christopher Tucker of Molland advertised that he no longer had financial responsibility for his wife Elizabeth since she left him.

1822 Four smugglers from the *Neptune* of Beer were sentenced to serve in the navy.

1823 It was reported that many Plymouth shop fronts were replaced in order to accommodate the installation of gas.

1932 The first recorded nightingale of the year was seen at Kingsteignton.

❧ 20 ❧

1626 A Northam woman was overheard calling her neighbour a whore and 'baggage whore'.

1721 Burial of John Hawkins, Mary Tavy blacksmith and wrestler.

onions was not got in last month, it must not be delayed after the beginning of this. Plant an early crop of potatoes the first fortnight and the main crop in the

APRIL

1829 Plums, cherries, sponge laurel, wood sorrel and dog violets were in bloom at Exeter.

1842 Veitch and Son offered from its nursery two new geraniums raised by J.B. Swete of Oxton House in Kenton. The first was Rose of Oxton which was 'a fine bright rose with a clear white centre' and the second was Mullata which was 'a beautiful clouded flower, upper petals being almost black, and the under petals deep crimson'.

❧ 21 ❧

Astrological Sign of TAURUS, the Bull
(through to May 20th)

1789 The body of a pilot, drowned seven weeks before, was found floating a mile off Exmouth Bar with his shoes and silver buckles on, spy glass in his coat pocket and watch in his fob.

1816 George Parker Bidder, the nine-year old Moretonhampstead boy billed as 'the calculating phenomenon', answered three questions in two minutes including 'how many drops are there in a pipe of wine, each cubic inch containing 4685 drops, each gallon containing 231 cubic inches, and each pipe containing 126 gallons?'

1845 William Nosworthy was transported overseas seven years for stealing four bags of apples in Highweek.

1922 Two hundred people came to the first annual dance of the Exeter Ping Pong League at Deller's Cafe in Exeter. Guest's Syncopated Orchestra provided music.

1949 Chinese communists fired on Devonport-manned HMS *Amethyst* and HMS *Consort* on the Yangtse River.

---

latter end of the month. Make the main sowing of hardy annuals. ✻ 1901 – *In the first fortnight plant the second early crop of potatoes, and the main crop*

APRIL

❧ 22 ❧

1615 Thomas Nyle was paid eleven shillings for two boat-loads of stones for the building of the Hospital of Orphans Aid in Plymouth.

1793 High grain prices prompted a riot at a grist mill near Crediton.

1829 Bank Holiday

1944 Children under 16 were not permitted to watch Constance Bennett in *Sin Town* in Exeter.

❧ 23 ❧

St George's Day

Birthday of James Anthony Froude, historian: born at Dartington, 1818.

1685 The church bells at Axminster were rung when James II was proclaimed king.

1686 At Powderham Castle one pound was given 'to Stroude the apothecary for bleeding my master with leeches'.

1789 An official national day of Thanksgiving to celebrate the recovery of George III was marked throughout Devon.

1829 The coaches arriving and leaving Exeter were decorated with evergreens and flags and the guards blew their bugles.

1832 It was reported that a Barnstaple lady was injured by a flower pot falling from a window.

1845 The foundation stone of the new church at Whimple was laid and inserted into the building was a bottle with an inscription, 'other particulars' and coins.

about the end of the month. Sow beans for succession. Sow red beetroot in the second week. About the same time sow borecole or Scotch greens and Brussels

APRIL

❧ 24 ❧

1591 Sir Francis Drake finished his great and lasting public work of bringing fresh water into Plymouth from Dartmoor. The Corporation celebrated with a civic dinner.

1827 A woman fell while gathering limpets and broke both legs and fractured her skull in Northam.

1900 The 'Great Russian Drama' *Denounced* played at the Theatre Royal, Exeter.

1922 A group of Australian bowlers visited Barnstaple.

❧ 25 ❧

Birthday of Joanna Southcott, visionary: born at Gittisham, 1750

1625 The mayor of Totnes paid 2 shillings to 'buy leather to make balls'.

1826 At Exeter's theatre appeared Mr Keene, 'an actor of colour who has attained such celebrity in the American Theatre as to be termed The African Roscius'.

1842 William E. Rendles' Union Road Nurseries in Plymouth offered Lyne's Circassian Geranium which, it was assured gardeners, had 'a first-rate character'.

❧ 26 ❧

1624 Hugh Vaughan was born and on his memorial stone in the parish church of Clyst Honiton is written:
Hugh son of Charles Vaughan esq.
Born 26 April 1624

sprouts. Sow lettuce for succession once a month. Plant in a shady place slips of sage, thyme, rue and other herbs. In the fruit garden proceed with grafting.

APRIL

Died 7 August 1631
Short though his life, eternal yet his rest
God takes them soonest whom he loveth best.

1793 A 'very hot press' recruited a great number of seamen in Plymouth.

1852 A gunpowder explosion destroyed a house in Newton Poppleford.

1929 The 3 elephants, 14 lions, 12 polar bears, 7 leopards, 10 zebras, 10 Bengal tigers, 10 bears, 200 monkeys, 20 apes, 2 hyenas, 2 pumas, 4 pelicans and 4 sea lions in Chapman's London Olympia Zoo performed at Exeter.

❧ 27 ❧

1603 Joan Morrishe of Silverton testified that a Torquay man climbed over the garden wall to demand food and claimed to be the King of England, Ireland, Scotland and France.

1829 It was reported that the old seating in Exeter Cathedral would be reused in a 'country' church now being altered and repaired.

1836 At the exhibition of the Devon County Floricultural Society Messrs Lucombe, Pince & Co. showed Chinese Azaleas, Rhododendrons and Camelias.

1852 At a meeting of the Useful Knowledge Society in Teignmouth a lecture was delivered on 'The Druids'.

1897 The audience was amused by 'Plantation Songs in Character' at a social evening held by the Youth Recreation Association in East Budleigh.

Make the main sowing of hardy annuals this month. ❊ *1907 – Sow whatever was omitted last month and plant out whatever pot herbs are ready for that*

APRIL

❧ 28 ❧

1871 The season's first oak and ash trees were seen in leaf in Zeal Monachorum.

1912 The *Lapland* came into Plymouth bringing 167 survivors from the wreck of the *Titanic*.

1922 Norton Brothers of Exeter had a 'Great End of Season' Gramophone Offer.

❧ 29 ❧

1829 Lady Smocks were flowering 'like silver by the brook sides' in Exeter.

1852 It was reported that an Exeter youth was caught in the theft of 25 lbs of potatoes because the variety, 'early Medlands', found in his possession was unusual to Exeter.

1858 Charlotte Cooksley, a Torquay prostitute, was sent to the House of Correction for 14 days for publicly using profane language.

1882 Chimneys and trees were pulled down in high winds throughout the county.

❧ 30 ❧

1657 Among the kitchen items purchased at Sydenham besides beef, veal, mutton and lamb were 3 quarts of gooseberries, 3 neats' tongues, 29 chickens, 6 pounds of beef tallow, 18 pounds of butter, a quart of rose water, 6 quarts of vinegar, 3 quarters of almonds, 150 apples, a bushel of samphire and 45 eggs.

purpose. Continue the sowing of asparagus, broccoli, Dutch turnip, German greens, nasturtiums, and savoys, and plant out rhubarb, seakale, artichokes

APRIL

1827   A blackbird in Stonehouse was reputedly imitating the song 'Hey the Bonnie Breast Knots'.

1845   Railway workers in South Brent were suspected of burning a furze break, of 20 acres, which was maintained for foxes.

1902   Opening of new premises of the Devonport Royal Sailors' Home.

JOHN REYNOLDS
IRONMONGER,
COAL & GENERAL MERCHANT,
CULLOMPTON.

COAL, COKE, FIREWOOD,
Salt, Manures, Linseed Cake,
Slate, Tile, Cement, &c.

AGRICULTURAL IMPLEMENTS
WRINGERS, MANGLES, LAWN MOWERS.

Lamps & Oil Stoves
PETROLEUM & BENZOLINE,
METHYLATED SPIRIT
LINSEED & MACHINE OIL.

GUNS & SPORTING AMMUNITION
TRAVELLING TRUNKS,
Stoves, Grates, & Kitchen Ranges.

IRON ROOFING & FENCING

CHEAPEST HOUSE IN THE CITY
FOR
PROVISIONS
LENDON BROS.,
90, FORE STREET, EXETER

Specialities :—

BACON   FINEST WILTSHIRE
(FIRST PRIZE MEDAL)

HAMS   FINEST YORK
FINEST WILTSHIRE
FINEST HOME-CURED

CHEESE   ENGLISH CHEDDAR
GORGONZOLA
STILTON
CANADIAN, &c.

ALL GOODS
AT
CO-OPERATIVE PRICES

and small salading. The young celery plants sown in February or March may be pricked out and others sown. Earth up peas, and water seedling beds. ❋❋❋

S. & J. PARNALL
SADDLERS
AND
HARNESS & MANUFACTURERS,
42 Old Town Street,
PLYMOUTH,
OPPOSITE PARK STREET.
LEGGINGS OF EVERY DESCRIPTION.
Branch Establishment at Roborough.

OPPOSITE ROYAL HOTEL.

J. JERGER,
(LATE ROBT. BURT.)
Practical Watch and Clock
MAKER,
GOLDSMITH & MANUFACTURING JEWELLER,
42 Fore Street, Devonport.
ENGLISH & FOREIGN WATCHES, CLOCKS & JEWELLERY
REPAIRED.

TO THE ADMIRALTY AND WAR DEPARTMENT.

LONG & Co.,
103 Union Street, PLYMOUTH,
ARCHITECTURAL, LANDSCAPE,
MARINE & PORTRAIT
PHOTOGRAPHERS.

Photographs of Her Majesty's Ships,
Can be had at this Establishment; also a great variety of
Views of the Neighbourhood, 1s. each,
MOUNTED or UNMOUNTED.
Photographic Portraits taken from 10 a.m. until dusk.
Cartes de Visites, from 4s. per Dozen.
CABINETS FROM 10/- PER DOZEN.
Sole Agents in Devonport for LONG & Co.'s Productions,
MESSRS. WOOD & TOZER, 49 Fore Street.

GEORGE J. POORE
Copper, Steel & Brass Plate
Visiting, Invitation & Business Cards, Bills of Parcels, Lading & Exchange
Arms, Crests & Cyphers in Gold, Silver, &c. Shop-cuts, Door Plates &c. made & Engraved
ENGRAVER & PRINTER,
LITHOGRAPHIC   Plymouth.   PRINTING OFFICE.

MAY

*In May get a weed-hook, a crotch and a glove,
and weed out such weeds, as the corn do not love.
For weeding of winter corn, now it is best;
but June is the better for weeding the rest.*

Thomas Tusser, 1557

MAY

❧ 1 ❧

Birthday of Thomas Mogford, painter: born at Exeter, 1809

1567 Morris Dancers performed in Plymouth.

1570 Robert Spry was paid six shillings and four pence for painting Plymouth's May Pole.

1604 The city authorities banned dogs from being kept within Exeter.

1823 Plymouth had an unofficial May Day parade at three in the morning with music provided by drums and cow horns.

1830 Opening of the Royal Union Baths, Plymouth.

1844 The first train steamed into Exeter's St David's station from London.

1852 Plans were being made to form a cricket club in Teignmouth.

1876 Opening of Agnes Weston's Sailors' Rest in Plymouth.

❧ 2 ❧

1768 Three soldiers were executed for raping a woman near Crediton.

1826 It was reported from Plymouth that some relics of antiquity were found during the renovations of St Andrew's Church including a carved oak screen and several ancient coins.

1827 The High Sheriff was the first to drive over the new Teignmouth to Shaldon Bridge.

1844 Crowds watched trains arrive at Exeter's St David's station and small boys went through the streets annoying and alarming locals by imitating the trains' whistles.

❀❀❀ 1891 – *Sow carrots, lettuces, spinach, peas, cauliflowers, red beet for pickling, and a full crop of French and kidney beans. Transplant winter greens,*

MAY

1859 Opening by Prince Albert of the Brunel Railway Bridge linking Devon with Cornwall.

1870 Snow fell on Dartmoor.

1880 Kissing Day at Torquay.

1964 Death of Lady Nancy Astor.

ও 3 ৬

1262 The Prior of Totnes made an agreement with a local man to clear the road to Follaton.

1560 Philip Larymer of Barnstaple had his two sons, both called John, baptised and buried.

1660 John Willoughby of Payhembury heard from London he would soon receive tulips and anemones and other plants 'that are rare and not common in every garden'.

1814 Exeter continued to celebrate the news of peace with bell-ringing, the decoration of shops and cannon-firing.

1829 A pair of false teeth, recently manufactured in Exeter, received high praise for their natural qualities.

1869 The Torquay Rowing Club was established.

1883 Death of the Reverend John Russell, the hunting parson, at Black Torrington.

1880 Sting Nettle Day at Bovey Tracey, children flogged one another with nettles.

1942 (3rd–4th) Thirty German aircraft flew up the Exe estuary in the early morning, under a Full Moon, and dropped fire bombs on Exeter for more than an hour causing utter devastation in more than 38 acres of the centre. In Germany it was claimed 'Exeter was a jewel and we have destroyed it'.

cauliflowers, lettuces, cabbages and celery. Hoe and stake peas. Plant out the plants potted last month, provided there is no appearance of frost. ❋ 1896 –

MAY

❧ 4 ❧

1601   Death of Peter Blundell, founder of the Tiverton school.

1837   Custom of hunting the Earl of [Ty]Rone at Combe Martin [last occasion]. The Earl (wearing a grotesque mask, smock stuffed with straw and a string of sea-biscuits round his neck) meandered on a donkey through the town accompanied by a Hobby Horse, Fool and troop of grenadiers.

1852   Death of the grandson of the owner of the Castle Inn, Totnes, from an accident while shooting blackbirds in Newfoundland.

❧ 5 ❧

1687   Burial of a Topsham man and his son in a single coffin.

1882   A Devonport policeman received an 'easy chair' upon his retirement.

1922   A nightingale was heard at New Cross in Kingsteignton.

❧ 6 ❧

Birthday of Henry Philpotts, Bishop of Exeter: born at Bridgwater, Somerset, 1778

1326   Hugh Coffin of Lynton acknowledged receiving 40 shillings from Forde Abbey.

1504   The Dartmouth Mayor's court decided Margaret Smyth and her daughter were 'common bawds'.

1569   A tumbler performed in Dartmouth.

1625   The mayor of Totnes gave six pence to a leper who came from Bath.

Hoe industriously all advancing crops. Sow peas for succession. Sow radishes, summer savoury, spinach, and broccoli. Thin out early horn? Carrots. Sow

MAY

1823 The *Mount-Stone* of Plymouth, en route to Newfoundland, was wrecked on an iceberg.

1926 Devon County Show was cancelled due to the General Strike.

1943 *Road to Morocco,* with Bob Hope, Bing Crosby and Dorothy Lamour, played at the Premier Cinema in Okehampton while Clark Gable and Lana Turner appeared in *Honky Tonk* at The Cinema in Holsworthy.

❧ 7 ❧

1646 Surrender of Fort Charles, Salcombe, the last Royalist stronghold in Devon.

1826 Measles were prevalent in Appledore.

1827 Rumours reached Exeter that the government planned to bring several thousand destitute Scots to farm Dartmoor.

1852 At a case of bigamy in Newton Abbot the second wife refused to press charges and the judge admonished the first wife 'not to interfere with her husband's happiness again'.

1852 Messrs Stephens & Co., Honiton lacemakers of Sidmouth and Otterton, provided tea for their 703 lacemakers.

1883 Mayor's Monday in Bovey Tracey.

1916 Snow fell at Princetown.

1926 At Newton St Cyres the tarmac caught fire while the road was being repaired.

❧ 8 ❧

1503 The Dartmouth Mayor's court decided John Peter, Joan Wynter, Joan Hew and Wilmot Reche all sold beer with a

cauliflowers to come into use in October, and plant out those raised in March. Loosen the surface soil about onions, and plant out the autumn-sown ones

MAY

froth and that Petronella Stone and Agnes Wellys were 'common gossips'.

1508 Petronella Stone was fined again for being a 'common gossip'.

1627 Robert Bellman of Cornwood was buried with the inscription placed on the monument to him and his widow (she died less than a fortnight earlier):

> *Here's rest and peace*
> *Within the grave*
> *Which we in life*
> *Could never have.*

1639 Broadhembury's vicar was accused of trying to put his hands up a woman's coat.

1836 Fire broke out in the Black Boy Beer & Cider shop in the parish of St Sidwells. Henry Honeychurch, the keeper, 'in a state of stupid drunkeness' was overheard to say 'Let it burn, it has been set on fire'.

1926 In the midst of the General Strike an angry Plymouth crowd, reported to be 15,000 strong, gathered to see whether the trams were working and were attacked with batons by plainsclothes and uniformed policemen.

❧ 9 ❦

1626 An Axminster baker tried to discover the identity of the thief who stole his lamb by measuring a foot print found at the scene of the crime. He suspected Edward Giles because his 'colour and countenance changed' when questioned but Giles fled before his shoe could be measured.

1738 Baptism at Dodbrooke of John Wolcot, poet, satirist, who later wrote under the sobriquet of Peter Pindar.

during the first moist weather. Keep an eye on insects and destroy them. ✱ *1898 –*
Plant out from seed bed, cabbage, broccoli, Brussels sprouts, and winter greens,

MAY

1793 The *Betsey*, *James* and *Increase*, three barges engaged in the coal trade from Starcross to Exeter, were advertised for sale by auction.

1847 A lecture was given on 'The Music and Musicians of Exeter' at the Exeter Scientific and Literary Institution.

1853 Opening of the Plymouth Sailors' Home.

1858 Bovey Tracey's Mock Lord Mayor Day

After the election the Lord Mayor and Lady Mayoress processed round the boundaries accompanied by more than one hundred horsemen.

❧ 10 ❦

1596 Hugh Beare was hanged outside the South Gate at Exeter for counterfeiting.

1792 One of the most productive pear harvests known in the county was expected.

1822 The 'Brighton Youth' ran 50 miles in 8 hours starting on Blackboy Road, Exeter.

1831 Two Godwits were seen at the Lara near Plymouth.

1869 Lightning struck a house in Plymouth.

1873 Laying of the foundation stone of The Wigwam, subsequently known as Oldway Mansion, in Torquay.

❧ 11 ❦

1660 Charles II was proclaimed King in Exeter at five public places

etc., prepare trenches for celery, do not wait for the moment you want them, sow a few rows of kidney beans. Sow small salads every week; radishes and lettuces

MAY

'with great solemnity during all which time the said conduits ran with wine...at night tar barrels and bonfires capered aloft – all which was done with the greatest expression of gladness that possibly could be imagined'.

1829 It was announced that a cock match would take place at Crab Tree in Plymouth for £100 a side, the best of 41 matches.

1829 A man was hit by his own gun while swallow-shooting on Haven Banks, Exeter.

1847 A food riot broke out in Cullompton.

1870 Distant thunder was heard in Plymouth all day.

1880 (11th–13th) The Devon County Rifle Assocation met at Ernesettle.

❧ 12 ❦

1581 Baptism of the son of Richard and Joan Troute in Barnstaple. Two years earlier Richard Troute denied breaking a marriage contract with another woman by cutting an apple in half and sharing it publicly to symbolise their betrothal but in the following months his accuser had an illegitimate son born.

1607 Earthquakes were felt in Barnstaple, Tiverton and Bampton.

1660 In Barnstaple Charles II was proclaimed King.

1823 Exeter's mayor interrupted a boxing match between 'Topsham Joe' and Henry Harris.

1829 The first lady birds of the year were spotted on plants in Exeter.

1858 An Exeter woman appeared before magistrates accused of attempting suicide.

thrice; spinach once a fortnight; carrots and onions for late drawing. Sow peas and beans, cauliflowers, &c, for late crops. Propagate by cuttings, dahlias,

MAY

1912 The First Devon Yeomanry, Territorials, National Reserve, Red Cross Society, Church Lads Brigade and the Boy Scouts were among those in the Sidmouth Church Parade.

❧ 13 ❧

1643 Alice Searle and Besse Randall, servants at Tawstock in north Devon, received one pound each as their half-yearly wages.

1858 A robin nested in a white broccoli in Paignton.

1926 Due to the General Strike only half of Exeter Tramways' service ran and a majority of Exeter's railwaymen refused to work until the union gave notice.

❧ 14 ❧

1847 Food riots occurred in Exeter.

1857 Among the prisoners committed to Devon County Prison were James Molland for misconduct in South Molton Workhouse (14 days), Thomas Smith for being absent from HMS *Ajax* (21 days) and Cornelius McCarthy for vagrancy at Highweek (28 days).

1881 The Plymouth Omnibus & Carrying Company extended its route to Millbay Station.

1926 The Cornwall Aviation Company offered airplane rides from Gallows' Field, Heavitree.

❧ 15 ❧

1611 Walter Yonge of Colyton wrote Devon had the driest springs 'as never was before seen or heard of'.

pansies, double wall-flowers, rockets, scarlet lychnis and lobelias by dividing the roots. ✽ *1900 – Hoe and thin parsnips and carrots. Sow long pod beans,*

MAY

1632 A Navy captain reported great panic caused by rumours of pirates at Seaton.

1829 Thieves stole two bags of potatoes from a potato-cave in Torrington and left behind a new pair of boots.

1839 Snow fell on Dartmoor.

1847 Some 2,000 tulips bloomed in a Tiverton garden.

1889 Upwards of 2,000 men, women and children at Bicton Park, and another 1,500 at Stevenstone, celebrated the marriage of Miss Gertrude Rolle to Lieutenant Hugh Drummond.

❧ 16 ❦

1793 In Exeter a portrait of the Prince of Wales was exhibited and reportedly 'leaves the mind in doubt whether it is life or not'.

1876 The American Decoy Rat Trap was sold at the Devon County Show.

1882 The site on the Hoe for Smeaton's Eddystone Lighthouse settled.

1883 *The Exeter Flying Post* applauded the Exeter Council's decision to reject Sunday closing of public houses on the grounds there would be an inevitable increase in barbers' shops in 'low neighbourhoods' (which would sell alcohol in inner rooms).

❧ 17 ❦

Birthday of Charles Fowler, architect: born at Cullompton, 1792

borecoles, Brussels sprouts, broccoli, and cabbage. Sow cauliflowers to come into use in October. Sow cress every week for succession in a moist situation, and

MAY

1525   Four pence was given to a Tiverton servant for bringing strawberries to the Countess of Devon.

1787   Strawberries, grapes, peaches, nectarines and figs were picked in Saltram's hothouses.

1814   In the procession at St Thomas celebrating peace was Napoleon in a cart with his 'brother in iniquity Monsieur Satan' going home to Elba.

1836   A gang of burglars was thought to have been captured in Witheridge.

1845   In Exeter Market mushrooms sold for one shilling per dozen, French beans were one shilling per hundred, rhubarb two pence per pound and gooseberries were four pence per quart.

1847   Food riots occurred in Exmouth and Torquay.

❧ 18 ❧

1565   Margaret Littlejohn of Whimple was accused of sorcery and chanting 'joint to joint, sinew to sinew and bone to bone and as green as grass and grass is it now'.

1829   One of the two men in a Crediton puglistic contest broke his neck and died.

1833   Some 3,000 tulips bloomed in Mr Townsend's garden in Rack Lane, Exeter.

1847   A 'mob' of women and children called for lower bread prices in Bideford.

1857   An inquest, held into the death of an infant girl found floating in a tributary of the Exe near St David's Station in Exeter, decided upon drowning or strangulation.

mustard every fortnight. Sow scarlet runner beans the first or second week. Sow annuals for late autumn flowering. Keep all advancing flower-stems neatly

MAY

❧ 19 ❧

Birthday of Lady Nancy Astor: in Virginia, 1879.

1686 A payment of ten shillings was made on behalf of Francis Courtenay of Powderham 'to Mr Hooper for giving my master a Vomit'.

1821 A covey of 12 partridges was seen at Sherwood near Exeter.

1833 A Peony Tree, with bright crimson blossom, was in full bloom in Mr Sclater's garden in Heavitree Road, Exeter.

1881 The King and Queen of Sweden visited Plymouth and the Dock Yard.

❧ 20 ❧

1789 An inquest was held at Plymouth into the death of a 70 year-old Jew by the name of Moses who was found on the Brethren Steps in a state of partial undress and next to a small knife with which, apparently, he 'had cut off his privities'.

1869 A meteor was seen at 9.15 p.m. in Great Torrington.

1880 The temperature reached 76° in Ashburton.

1916 A meteor was seen across Devon a few minutes after 8 pm.

1930 *The Devon and Exeter Gazette* argued for speed limits for motor cars in Exeter.

1978 The North Devon coast path was officially opened.

❧ 21 ❧

Astrological Sign of GEMINI, the Twins
(through to June 20th)

1616 Burial at Exeter of 'Mother Warren, an old woman'.

tied. Propagate by cuttings double wallflowers, rockets, etc. ✤ *1901 – Hoe industriously all advancing crops. Sow radishes, summer savoury, spinach, and*

MAY

1819 Northleigh's rector was accused of adultery with a Colyton woman.

1836 It was reported that William Melhuish of Upton Pyne won Best Sheep Shearer at the Devon Agricultural Society show.

1846 First exhibition of the Torbay Horticultural Society.

1866 John Goss of Cullompton was fined ten shillings for driving a bread cart without weights or measures.

1875 The Devon County Agricultural Association held their show at Newton Abbot but the Dog Show elicited great criticism in *The Exeter & Plymouth Gazette* with Hamlet II (a large pointer) receiving rare praise.

1949 A live 500 pound German bomb was found in Plymouth.

❧ 22 ❦

Birthday of W.G. Hoskins, historian: born at Exeter, 1908

1432 Dartmouth men robbed a Dunkirk vessel off the Brittany coast.

1610 Exeter officials gave sugar loaves to two canons in appreciation for the cathedral's morning lectures.

1620 Philip Jarman of Exeter was cited by the city scavengers for having a dung heap at his back door, Mrs Dorothy Cranbury for 'filth' lying before her door and William Heath for a 'heap of dirt before his shop'.

1767 Four medical doctors testified that Exeter was free of infectious disease in spite of the recent deaths of twelve people.

1835 A public lecture on 'Optics, vision & colour' with views of

broccoli. Thin out early horn Carrots. Sow cauliflowers to come into use in October, and plant out those raised in March. Loosen the surface soil about

MAY

Stonehenge, the Holy Sepulchre at Jerusalem, Mount Vesuvius and Pompeii was given at Teignmouth.

1858   A Bee-eater was shot near Malborough.

1881   The Salvation Army's meeting at the Devonport Institute ended in panic when it was discovered that a saboteur had cut a gas pipe.

1950   The first woman was elected Lord Mayor of Plymouth.

❧ 23 ❦

1782   An influenza outbreak hit South Devon.

1857   Richards' Cantharides Pomade for 'producing hair on bald places' was available at The Original Shampooing Rooms, Exeter.

1890   Eighteen children received prizes for 'Best collections of passages from the Bible relating to kindness to animals' at the annual meeting of the Budleigh Salterton branch of the Band of Mercy.

❧ 24 ❦

Birthday of James Veitch, the third in that line of Exeter nurserymen: near Exeter, 1815.

Birthday of Edmund Turner Pearse who lived to be 105 years old: born at North Petherwin, 1815.

1756   A flock of newly-introduced Newfoundland geese caused destruction in a Lympstone garden.

onions, and plant out the autumn-sown ones during the first moist weather. Keep an eye on insects and destroy them. ❀ 1904 – *Sow peas and beans,*

MAY

1821   At Exeter a black man failed to run barefoot the distance of nine miles within an hour by 3½ minutes but was rewarded with the sum of three pounds.

1821   John Pike of Colaton Raleigh was drowned while eel fishing in the river Otter.

1822   An Egyptian mummy was auctioned for £435 in Plymouth for non-payment of customs duty.

1890   A tornado hit the town of Tiverton with thunder, lightning, rain and hailstones – flooding caused some £1,000 worth of damage to the borough's highways.

❧ 25 ❧

Birthday of Sir Thomas Acland: born at Killerton, 1809.

1782   On one man's memorial stone in Portlemouth it was inscribed:

> *Through poison strong he was cut off,*
> *And brought to death at last,*
> *It was by his apprentice girl,*
> *On whom there's sentence past,*
> *O may all people warning take,*
> *For she was burned to a stake!*

1828   Whitsun. Scarlet Day (Plymouth). The Mayor and Council attended divine service in their scarlet robes.

1829   It was rumoured in Barnstaple that a body snatcher was in the town.

1852   Police were called at a fracas which broke out over treatment given several children who were trying to peep under the canvas at Hengler's Circus in Exeter.

cauliflowers, cabbages, Brussels sprouts, etc. Peas that are in progress must be staked. Keep down weeds and maintain war against caterpillars and other pests

MAY

❧ 26 ❧

1821　Several inches of snow fell on Dartmoor and Exmoor.

1870　The water quality of the river Exe near its junction with the river Culm was judged to be 'slightly turbid'.

1880　Rain ended the drought at East Budleigh.

1895　Two straw ricks were destroyed by fire in Uplowman.

1930　The columnist 'Molly', in *The Devon & Exeter Gazette*, advised women that 'the days of buttons and button holes in women's garments are passing and elastic is taking their place'.

❧ 27 ❧

1598　Alice Magridge of Tiverton was suspected of assisting an abortion by asking for 'a medicine for a woman's griefs'.

1836　A dog, thought to have bitten a pig and suspected to be rabid, was shot near Exwick.

1849　Five Exeter coffee shops were under police surveillance including one kept by Fanny Way in which on one occasion were 19 men and 4 prostitutes.

1882　The Exeter Vegetarian Society was formed.

1901　Whit-Monday. The Exeter Cart Horse Parade was held.

1977　Opening of the M5 to Plymouth.

❧ 28 ❧

Birthday of William Jackson, musician and Exeter Cathedral Organist: born at Exeter, 1730.

Birthday of John Smeaton, engineer of the third Eddystone Lighthouse: near Leeds, 1724.

of the garden. Plant out annuals raised in pots, and sow annuals for succession. Propagate by cuttings dahlias, pansies, double wall flowers, rockets, scarlet lychnis;

MAY

1522 Robert Derkeham, organist, was contracted at Buckland Abbey to teach music and organ-playing as well as assist the choir for the yearly sum of £2 13s 4d, board, lodging and one new gown.

1821 National Census taken. It was reported that at Plymouth a head of household recorded his family stood at 2 guns and 3 pistols (his name was Gun and he had 3 children).

1822 William Pitt's birthday was celebrated by a dinner at The Hotel in Exeter with 'the utmost hilarity and good humour'.

1822 Wrestling and single-stick bouts at the Plympton St Maurice Fair attracted a number of 'ladies' who, it was claimed, merely pretended to avert their eyes when the men stripped 'and had their bodies indecently exposed'.

1878 Sidmouth residents near the railway station feared an owl's nightly attacks.

❧ 29 ☙

1585 English vessels and crews were seized in Spain; Barnstaple claimed losses of £6,000, Exeter £2,600 and Plymouth £3,500.

1660 Restoration Day / Royal Oak Day. In Plymouth's Great Black Book it was noted that Charles II 'to the great joy of the nation arrived at London the 29th of May, his birthday, and was proclaimed in this town with great triumph, the conduits running two days with wine, and shortly after a curious present of rare wroughted plate was presented his Majesty by this Corporation'.

1661, 1662, 1664, 1665, 1666, 1675, 1678, 1683, 1685, 1687 The church bells at Axminster were rung to mark the birthday of Charles II.

and lobelias by dividing the roots. Herbaceous border plants should be thinned out and staked. ✸ *1907 – Sow carrots, lettuces, spinach, peas, cauliflowers, red*

MAY

1744 Lawless Day. Young Exeter boys splashed passers-by who did not pay a fee.

1815 The William Pitt Club met in Exeter to celebrate Mr Pitt's birthday.

1829 Oak boughs thickly decorated Exeter houses.

1856 A Peace Parade marched through Exeter to celebrate the end of the Crimean War.

❧ 30 ❧

1821 Charles Alfred Stothard, a visiting London artist who was drawing a figure in a stained-glass window in Bere Ferrers' Church, fell from a ladder and died.

1823 A swarm of bees set upon a farmer's cart in Fore Street in Exeter.

1852 The activities of the Female Benefit Society at Axminster were called into doubt; after church their dance in the ballroom of the George became more public than was regarded appropriate.

1911 No rain fell in Sidmouth for the following sixteen days.

1930 A memorial was erected at Plymouth by the American Society of the Daughters of 1812 to note the humane care received locally by the crew of U.S.N. brig *Argus* after action in the Channel in 1813.

❧ 31 ❧

1617 Burial at Plymouth of Thomas Flickett of Lynn who was described as 'of Sir Walter Raleigh's ship'.

beet for pickling, and a full crop of French and kidney beans. Transplant winter greens, cauliflowers, lettuces, cabbages, and celery. Hoe and stake peas, propagate

MAY

1869 A bright red meteor with a red tail was seen from Torquay.

1882 An editorial in *Trewman's Exeter Flying Post* questioned how appropriate it was for the Bishop to support the erection of a statue to Charles Darwin.

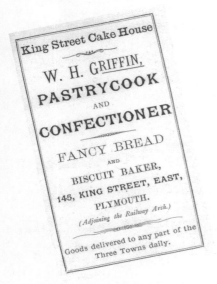

aromatic plants by means of slips or cuttings. Plant out the flowers potted last month. Protect from wind and rain ranunculuses, anemones, and tulips. ❊❊❊

JUNE

Copious dispenser of delight, bright June,
All hail! the meadows smile with flowery pride,
Shed from they lavish hand; the garden blooms;
Hills lift their verdant heads, and Nature joys,
To long lost honours, and to health restored!

John Bidlake, Plymouth, 1813

JUNE

❧ 1 ❧

1894 Opening of the Princess Gardens in Torquay by the Mayoress.

1895 There was talk in East Budleigh over artificial flowers being allowed in the churchyard.

1942 Exeter's Theatre Royal reopened with a performance of the Anglo-Polish Ballet.

❧ 2 ❧

1608 Four pirates were executed at Plymouth.

1609 Sir Thomas Gates left Plymouth in a fleet of 9 ships carrying 600 colonists for Virginia.

1782 Widespread disease was reported throughout Plymouth.

1821 An Exmouth cleric threatened to prosecute women who bathed in the sea on Sundays.

1828 Mrs Shaw of Stonehouse exhibited an oil painting of flowers at the Society of Arts in London and was awarded the gold Isis medal.

1873 The water supply for Stonehouse was rated as being 'slightly turbid, palatable'.

❧ 3 ❧

1653 The Reverend Thomas Larkham of Tavistock picked his first rose of the year.

1833 A show of Turkey Ranunculuses, which won three prizes, were displayed in an Exeter window for the week.

❀❀❀ 1891 – *Continue sowing such vegetables as were directed last month; sow turnips for winter use. Plant out savoys, celery, cabbages, broccoli, cauli-*

JUNE

1882 Queen's Birthday: thousands watched a Grand Review in Devonport Park.

1934 Three stormy petrels were seen between Morte Point and Lundy Island.

࣓ 4 ࣓

1629 Mary Melhuish of Merton complained that she was slandered by Agnes Payne saying to her 'thou art a mare and thou hast a **** like a mare'.

1792 The foundation stone of Floretta Dock was laid by John Seale at Dartmouth and afterwards a large party processed to a castle in the pleasure grounds of Mount Boone where a bullock was roasted and after rural dances, balls and fireworks 'Signor Rosignol entertained by visiting bushes and shrubberies in the gardens and imitating most ingeniously the feathered tribe'.

1827 A correspondent in *The Alfred – West of England Journal* warned hunters fond of rook pies not to place the dead birds in their pockets due to vermin.

1839 Citrons and lemons grown by Mrs Lane in a Totnes greenhouse were shown at the London Horticultural Society exhibition and won a Banksian medal.

1852 Two Exeter fish vendors, Jane Screech and Jane Reed, quarreled over some fish which resulted in Screech serving a two-day sentence in prison for hitting Reed in the face.

࣓ 5 ࣓

1432 The mayor of Exeter and five other men enquired into the illegal seizure of French cloth and wine.

---

flowers. ✽ 1896 – *Make the last sowing of peas and beans for the season. Sow radish and lettuce for succession. A main sowing of turnips may now be made.*

JUNE

1731 The third of the great fires of Tiverton began in a baker's house.

1876 Mr J.C. Buckmaster of the South Kensington Museum, gave a lecture on 'Food and Cookery' at Crediton as part of an attempt to establish a School of Cookery in the town.

1889 The Devon County Dog Show Society exhibited at the Bath and West of England Show at Exeter. Among the winners were The Black Prince (Newfoundland, challenge class) and Ivanhoe (Great Dane, Open Class).

1917 Luminous rain fell at Tavistock at 11.30 pm.

1929 Complaints were made in Exmouth of the Sunday sixpenny excursionists from Exeter who became intoxicated and 'went about the streets looking up at the windows shouting rude remarks'.

❧ 6 ❧

Birthday of Captain Robert Scott, Polar explorer: born at Devonport, 1868

1605 An Admiralty Court was held in Barnstaple.

1651 Martha Berney, a north Devon washing woman, was paid 6 shillings for her 6 months' wages.

1750 Baptism of Joanna Southcott, visionary, at Ottery St Mary.

1825 A burning tar barrel and effigy of a local brushmaker, who had the cognomen of 'Lily' and had falsely accused a woman of stealing, was carried through Ashburton and lit in the market place.

1944 D-Day. As part of Operation Overlord, Plymouth Command worked with the American forces who left from Brixham,

Thin carrots, hoeing deeply among them at the same time. Earth up celery. Sow cream-coloured kidney beans. Earth up potatoes afterwards. Destroy the black

JUNE

Dartmouth, Plymouth, Salcombe and Torquay for Utah Beach.

❧ 7 ❧

Birthday of R.D. Blackmore, author of *Lorna Doone*: born at Longworth, Berkshire, 1825.

1561   James Cooke sat in the pillory at Exeter for having picked pockets.

1585   Captain John Davis left Dartmouth in the *Sunshine* of London accompanied by the *Moonshine* of Dartmouth in the hope of discovering the North West Passage.

1757   A swarm of bees set upon Queen Anne's statue in the Walk in Barnstaple.

1823   A Nightingale was heard on the banks of the Teign.

❧ 8 ❧

1589   William Dillon, who died 'of a wound that he gave unto himself in cutting of his throat but living after the same for the space of 15 days [and] showed forth most lively fruits of his repentance', was buried in Wear Giffard.

1792   Fire destroyed several houses in New Street, Moreton-hampstead.

1812   Fire in one of the rope-houses at Plymouth Dock caused an estimate £15,000 worth of damage.

1827   The *London* was launched at Haven Banks near Exeter.

1945   Gary Cooper and Ingrid Bergman featured in *For Whom the Bells Tolls* at the Premier Cinema, Okehampton.

fly on cherry-trees, &c. Tender annuals sown in pots may be planted in the open borders. Hoe and rake shrubberies frequently. ❀1898 – *Sow peas and beans for*

JUNE

❧ 9 ❧

1792 A mason fell from scaffolding in Plymouth and 'was dashed to pieces'.

1829 It was reported that three 'Cactus *speciossinus*', with several hundred blossoms, and two 'Cactus *speciosus*', with more than two thousand blossoms, attracted attention at two Exeter nurseries.

1845 A married man 'old enough to have known better' indulged in 'a free conversation' with a 'very free female' in Exeter's Mint Lane and was robbed of his purse containing some eleven pounds.

1895 A fox killed 11 fowls, including 2 hens and 5 turkeys, in Clayhanger.

1925 It was reported that Exeter was free of foot and mouth disease.

❧ 10 ❧

Birthday of Frederick Richard Lee, landscape painter: born at Barnstaple, 1798.

1626 Death of Valentine Carey, bishop of Exeter, after having ministered through the plague epidemic at Exeter finally caught the disease when it was thought to have ended.

1826 Lightning struck Alphington's church tower and killed a boy working there.

1839 Two otters, one weighing 30 pounds, were killed by the Copplestone Cross hounds at Upton Pynes.

1878 The Paris Exhibition drew away members of the Star Bicycle Club from a race to Dawlish.

late crops. Sow salading every ten days: also carrots and onions for drawing young. Pull and store winter onions if ripe. Train and prune the summer shoots

JUNE

1878 Nearly 3,000 persons visited the Royal Albert Memorial Museum in Exeter and only two of them were reported to be drunk.

❧ 11 ❧

1607 It was noted that on 'this day fell in Colyton, not far from the town, being as it seemed a thunder shower, and some thunder heard withal, among which were certain drops fell like blood, which stained those things as it fell on'.

1792 A Bideford man chopped off his thumb while cutting bark.

1827 It was reported that the Horticultural Society of London gave the Banksian Medal to the owner of Combe Royal near Kingsbridge for his orange, lemon and citron specimens.

1829 (11th–12th) A wrestling match took place in Tiverton.

1870 A public meeting in Torquay decided that bathing at Anstey's Cove was permitted only from sunrise to 1.30pm and that no gentleman could bathe, at any time, within sight of the ladies' beach.

❧ 12 ❧

Birthday of Charles Kingsley, author of *Westward Ho!:* born at Holne, 1819.

1616 Pocahontas arrived in Plymouth, with Uttamatomakkin, her father's councillor.

1823 For a wager of two glasses of gin a Sheriff's officer at Dartmouth consumed 52 raw eggs in 13½ minutes.

1866 A group of 300 persons gathered at Diptford for cockfighting but the event was stopped by the arrival of 4 constables.

of all descriptions of wall and trellis trees. Net over cherry trees to protect them from birds. Take up bulbs and tuberous roots, and dry them in the shade before

JUNE

1870 Following the death of Charles Dickens on the 9th, the Reverend W. Binns lectured at Devonport on 'Charles Dickens, considered as a teacher of ethics and religion'.

1895 Two pitchers filled with early Stuart coins were found in a Witheridge hedge.

❧ 13 ❧

1602 William Honeywell of Rydon went to church at Trusham in the afternoon and then spent the rest of the day playing bowls.

1623 Sir John Eliot, Vice Admiral of Devon, was instructed to send Captain John Nutt, a pirate in his custody, from Dartmouth to London for questioning.

1772 Captain James Cook sailed from Plymouth on the *Resolution* for the Antarctic.

1895 The Bishop of Sarawak opened a fete at Tidcombe House, Tiverton, for the Church of England Zenana Mission.

❧ 14 ❧

Birthday of George Parker Bidder, the 'calculating boy': Moretonhampstead, 1806

1845 The *Great Britain* arrived at Plymouth.

1870 A newly-wed man committed suicide at the railway station in Dawlish.

1895 It was reported that women would replace male junior clerks at the Post Office in Newton Abbot.

removing them. Remove all kinds of decaying crops. ❀ *1900 – Sow the last crop of early long pod beans. Plant out broccoli; thin carrots; sow cream coloured*

JUNE

❧ 15 ❧

1619 Baptism at Plymouth 'Fardinando Paleolagus, son of Theodore, an Italian' who was later noted as being Greek and of the Imperial Line.

1829 The scarlet pimpernel, known as 'the poor man's weather glass' because it opened and closed with wet weather, was in flower in Exeter.

1881 The Free Spiritual Society held a tea and social meeting in Plymouth.

❧ 16 ❧

Birthday of Princess Henrietta, daughter of Charles I: born at Exeter, 1644.

1628 The Deputy Lieutenants sought to have a fort erected at Sidmouth because of the French privateers on the coast.

1631 Thomas Heywood printed *The Fair Maid of the West* in which Bess Bridges, a Plymouth bar-maid, searches for love and finds Turkish pirates.

1656 Christobell Towill allegedly said she would cut the throat of Oliver Cromwell if he came to Exeter because he was to blame for the king's beheading.

❧ 17 ❧

1567 Baptism of Thomas Westcote, one of Devon's first historians, in Shobrooke.

1843 Messrs. Lucombe, Pince & Co. of St Thomas was awarded

kidney beans. Hoe between onions, and keep free from weeds. Make the last sowing of peas for the season. Water strawberries if necessary. Some of the quick-

JUNE

the Gold Banksian Medal for 21 new seedling hybrid heathers.

1845 The Exeter Express Train, which normally ran from Paddington to Exeter in 4½ hours, had an accident near Slough. Among the passengers was Mrs Davy of Honiton, lace-maker to the Queen and another woman who was so alarmed at the danger that 'it was doubtful whether she would ever be restored to the condition of a rational being'.

1870 Mr Rossiter, chemist at Tiverton, offered for sale 'Mrs Harris Herbert's American Hairdressing'.

1927 A number of laundered items were stolen from the Newton Abbot Steam Laundry but it was reported in *The Western Times* that the police 'have the matter in hand'.

❧ 18 ❧

1640 The *Elizabeth* of Plymouth returned after being attacked for nearly 8 hours by Barbary pirates. During the fight the English shouted 'come aboard you dogs if you dare' and held up some pork to them calling 'as it were in a merry or jeering way, to come aboard of their ship to eat some pork'.

1869 Twenty-five days of no rain ended at Torquay.

1875 The first rose show was held in Northernhay Gardens in Exeter.

❧ 19 ❧

1640 Four crewmen from the *Elizabeth*, slain while defending their ship from pirates, were buried.

1649 Robert Grincking, clockmaker, was given thirty shillings for

flowering annuals may yet be sown. Bulbs of ranunculus, hyacinths, anemones, and tulips must be taken up as soon as the foliage turns yellow. ❀ 1901 – *Make*

JUNE

repairing Exeter Cathedral's clock and a contract for ten shillings yearly for maintaining it.

1845 Mr Batty's Troop of Equestrians, accompanied by Mr White and his trained collection of animals and a band of musicians, paraded through Moretonhampstead.

1915 A recruiting advert was placed in *The Exeter Flying Post* that 'These boys didn't shirk, they want help! Listen for a moment – can't you hear them calling to you? Be a Man. There's a king's uniform waiting for you, go and put it on now.'

❧ 20 ❧

1242 The Bishop of Norwich granted an indulgence of 35 days for visits to Exeter's Cathedral.

1586 Nineteen pence was spent on fish for labourers digging ditches for Plymouth's defence.

1839 A severe thunderstorm, which struck Exeter and Teignmouth early in the evening, turned the sky a dark green, flooded the streets and hail broke windows.

1887 Devon, like the rest of the country, celebrated the Queen's Jubilee. In Tiverton there was a week of entertainments: a concert was given by the Musical Society, the Town Band played the National Anthem at various points throughout the town, the Society of Change-Ringers had a Jubilee 'Touch', bonfires were lit, and there were several public processions including by torch-light.

1922 The Prince of Wales sailed on the *Renown* into Plymouth harbour at the end of his eight-month world cruise.

1929 Madeleine Carroll featured in *What Money Can Buy* at the Palladium in Exeter.

the last sowing of peas and beans for the season. Sow radish and lettuce for succession. A main sowing of turnips may now be made. Thin carrots, hoeing

JUNE

❧ 21 ❦

Astrological Sign of CANCER, the Crab
(through to July 23rd)

1765 The curate of Brixton defended himself of charges of drunkeness and immorality.

1810 All 68 prisoners of the Devon County House of Correction were employed.

1823 It was reported from Plymouth that 'the friends of humanity will be delighted to hear' that Royal Marine Corps' punishment by cat-o'nine-tails had been replaced by the treadmill.

1831 It was reported that more than 500 'of the geranium tribe' were blooming at Powderham Castle.

1889 More than 70 Dartmouth inhabitants petitioned against the destruction of the Butterwalk for a new post office.

❧ 22 ❦

1613 Northernhay in Exeter, which had recently been levelled as a 'pleasant walk', was given public seats making this one of the earliest uses of public space as a 'park'.

1822 A thunderstorm swept through south Devon.

1828 Lightning struck Kingsbridge church.

1846 Death of Benjamin R. Haydon, Devon painter.

1866 Fifteen eggs cost one shilling in Exeter market.

1875 A nightingale was heard in Whitestone between noon and two o'clock in the afternoon.

deeply among them at the same time. Earth up celery. Sow cream-coloured kidney beans. Earth up potatoes afterwards. Destroy the black fly on cherry-trees, &c.

JUNE

❧ 23 ❦
Midsummer's Eve

1685   Richard Ward, a soldier who may have been involved with the landing of the Duke of Monmouth, died at the Dolphin Inn at Honiton.

1821   Laying of the foundation stone of the town hall at Plymouth Dock.

1822   Fire destroyed a house in Musbury.

1876   Pinder & Tuckwell of Exeter offered 2 pairs of tweed trousers, all wool, well-shrunk and made to order, for 26 shillings.

❧ 24 ❦
Quarter Day (Nativity of St John the Baptist)
Midsummer Day

1789   Exeter residents were warned against sleeping in rooms with bouquets of hawthorn (due to their causing headaches and fevers).

1824   Plymouth was in a building boom with more than 290 houses being built.

1899   £110 8s 9d was raised in Plymouth for Waif Saturday.

1929   Adolphe Menjou and Evelyn Brent featured in *A Night of Mystery* at King's Picture House in St Thomas and British Talkies were advertised as appearing 'very soon'.

1944   Members of Exeter City Council were angry that five women were appointed to the police force.

Tender annuals sown in pots may be planted in the open borders. Hoe and rake shrubberies frequently. ❀ 1907 – *Continue sowing such vegetables as were*

JUNE

❧ 25 ❧

1829 An ox trampled a small child to death in Exmouth and was shot on the beach.

1870 A man claiming to be King Theodore of Abyssinia was taken to the county asylum.

1875 It was reported that the *Ark* discovered an artillery target floating off Mortehoe.

❧ 26 ❧

1770 The Globe Inn at Exmouth reopened with a new bowling green.

1821 Fire destroyed Hele Paper Mills in Bradninch.

1822 At dusk a 'Cactus *Grandiflorus*' was in full bloom in an Exeter hot-house.

1845 Restoration work on Northernhay Gardens in Exeter was nearly completed.

1875 Budleigh Salterton had a disappointing mackerel season.

❧ 27 ❧

1602 A Portuguese prize ship was diverted from Plymouth because it was a 'pilfering town'.

1889 A public meeting in Paignton discussed preserving the Bishop's Palace and Tower.

1929 The Mount Radford Pharmacy in Exeter sold Marienbad Anti-Obesity Tablets.

directed last month; sow also turnips for winter use. Plant out savoys, celery, cabbages, broccoli, cauliflowers in shady borders, lettuces, leeks, cucumbers for

JUNE

〜 28 〜

1649 Noxious gas or vapours killed 2 men from St Sidwell's parish; they died 'with a damp of the well at the sign of the White Hart in South Gate Street'.

1833 For a wager Mr Richard Morris of Broadclyst caught, tied and sheared 60 sheep.

1837 An unusually coloured vole was captured in a hay field in Yealmpton.

1838 The Great Western Canal was fully opened.

1870 The Queen's Coronation Day was observed at Honiton as 'an almost general' holiday.

〜 29 〜

St Peter's Day

1228 The Dean and Chapter of Exeter reached an agreement with the Abbey and Convent of Buckfastleigh regarding the fishery at Staverton.

1626 The Commissioners appointed to look after affairs in Plymouth during the war wrote to the Privy Council that plague was so widespread they could not meet in safety.

1773 The rector of Bideford was accused of brawling in church.

1822 Plymouth's streets were unusually full of sailors spending their wages on hackney coaches and 'Polls'.

1871 An afternoon thunderstorm hit Ashburton.

1944 Basil Rathbone appeared in *The Hound of the Baskervilles* at the Gaumont, Exeter.

pickling; watering must be seen to in dry weather, and also the hoeing of cabbages, potatoes and peas. Thin out onions, parsnips, carrots and early turnips. Shade

JUNE

❧ 30 ❧

Birthday of John Day, author of *The Beggars' Opera*: born at Barnstaple, 1685.

1600 Prodigious catches of herring were caught along the north Devon coast. Throughout the month 'such multitudes of herrings came so near the shore at Clovelly Quay and all other those places, that the people went with that small provision of nets they had and took and drew them up the land in such plenty that they were sold for four shillings the thousand, the number of a barrel, and were such store that they gave them to their hogs to eat, and buried the rest in the ground, for lack of salt and barrels to preserve them'.

1630 A navy captain wrote from Plymouth that Egypt was never more infested with caterpillars than the Land's End was with pirates.

1770 Four young men drowned while bathing at Budleigh Salterton.

1819 It was announced that Joseph Congdon, of the Commercial Hotel in Plymouth, had purchased The Hotel in Exeter and would improve and repair the Ball and Card Rooms.

1828 A Dawlish house collapsed and fell into Upper Brook Street with its inhabitants (who were unharmed).

1831 Sidmouth prepared for a visit from Grand Duchess Helene of Russia.

1944 It was reported that Bridgerule raised £3,626 during Salute the Soldier Week.

and air melon plants and strike by cuttings double wallflowers, scarlet lychnis, rockets and stocks. Transplant annuals, biennials, and perennials. ✹ ✹

JULY

No tempest, good July,
Lest all things look ruly.

Thomas Tusser, 1557

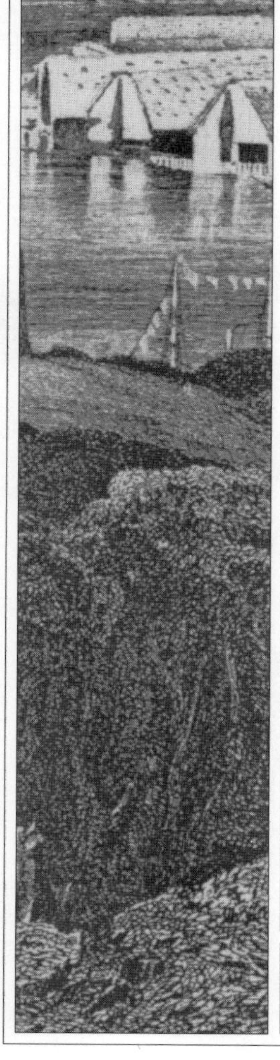

JULY

1

1629 Maude Somter, a Totnes widow, was ordered to stop selling cider.

1833 Among the sheep-shearers helping Richard Palk of Ipplepen were nine grandchildren and one great-grandchild.

1845 A 'cactus *grandiflora*' (?*Selenicereus grandiflorus*) bloomed in a hothouse belonging to John Newcombe of Starcross.

1870 It was announced that telegraph poles were erected in Sidmouth.

1911 (1st–28th) No rain fell in Sidmouth.

2

1549 Exeter's gates were shut to the several thousand Prayer Book rebels who besieged the city.

1688 Bonfires were lit in Exeter at the East and West Gates and in Cathedral Yard to support the acquittal of sedition charges against the Archbishop of Canterbury and six other bishops. Neither the fires or the abusive names such as 'Popish rogues' were welcomed by the mayor who tried to disperse the crowd.

1823 In the morning a Plymouth marine was found dead after drinking a bottle of rum in one draught for a wager the previous night.

1845 It was reported that the *Wilberforce* brought a cargo of African guano to Exeter.

1920 'Good old pickled boots' were available by post from Okehampton.

❁❁❁ 1891 – *Prepare all unoccupied ground for autumn and winter crops. Continue sowing radishes, lettuces, and turnips. Plant out broccoli, savoys,*

JULY

❧ 3 ❧
(3rd–August 11th) Dog Days

1635 Gregory Woolcott was alleged to have slandered John Loone of Exeter by calling him a whoremonger, whoremaster and 'whoremongering slave'.

1845 A game of skittles, the 'very healthy and manly recreation', was played for a wager of one sovereign at the Worth Arms in Tiverton.

1889 The Barnstaple Horse Show was held in the grounds of Pilton House.

1895 A Braunton woman was charged with stealing three cabbages.

❧ 4 ❧

1608 Frances Moor was apprenticed for nine years to Abraham Clarke, silkweaver of Plymouth, to 'instruct her in the best manner he can to make bone lace'.

1889 The German corvette *Ariadne* was in Dartmouth with boys training as seamen for the German navy.

1936 The Devon branch of the English Folk Dance and Song Society performed a festival of rustic dancing at the Bishops' Palace, Exeter.

❧ 5 ❧

1649 John Taylor, The Water Poet, walked seven miles to Barnstaple, 'a very fine sweet town, so clean and neat that in the worse of weather a man may walk the streets and never foul shoe or boot'.

leeks, cauliflowers, and winter cabbages, and earth up celery. Gather medicinal flowers and sweet herbs when in bloom, dressing them in the shade for winter

JULY

1767 Customs Official seized ten horse loads of French salt at Paignton.

1831 At Exeter J. Millman, 20, was transported overseas for 14 years for stealing bacon as was M. Viner, 24, for stealing a shawl.

1888 A public lunch in the Drill Hall followed the official opening of Tiverton's People's Park.

❧ 6 ❧

1822 A reward of twenty pounds was offered for the capture of a wild blackbird who imitated the crowing of a bantam at South Brent.

1824 The first pilchards of the season were caught off the Eddystone.

1874 Among the winners of the Budleigh Salterton & East Budleigh Garden Society Show were Susan Pyle (cleanest and neatest cottage) and H. Ellis (greatest number of wasp's nests).

1899 The 70 trained horses, 3 herds of elephants, 50 acrobats, 50 aerialists, 12 champion male and female equestrians, lady clowns, lady ringmasters and lady object holders of Barnum and Bailey, the 'Greatest Show on Earth', performed on Camp Field, Wonford.

1940 Plymouth had its first German bomb of the Second World War.

1948 *Fanny by Gaslight* played at the Savoy in Exeter.

---

use. ❀ *1896 – Earth up and stick peas, and earth up and top advancing beans. Plant the main crop of celery the first suitable weather. Sow lettuce for*

JULY

❧ 7 ❧
Translation of St Thomas Becket

1821　Jacob Lovelace's famous Exeter Clock was on public show in Exeter.

1828　An Exeter man was committed to the City Gaol on the charge of intending to rape a seven-year old child.

1836　In Ashburton a man by the name of MacDougal covered 170 feet in 16 hops.

1882　The Jubilee of the Reform Act was celebrated in Plymouth and a tablet was erected in the Bull Ring.

1940　Late in the afternoon Plymouth suffered its second serious bombing.

❧ 8 ❧

1208　An agreement was made to establish the boundaries of the parish of Lynton.

1870　It was reported in *The Devon Weekly Times* that newly-built Knightshayes near Tiverton 'possesses the advantage of an elevated position and a series of very beautiful views of the surrounding countryside'.

1870　A thunderstorm hit Ashburton at 10.15 at night.

1907　Simmons Park in Okehampton was officially opened.

❧ 9 ❧

Birthday of W. Keble Martin, botanist: born at Radley, Oxfordshire, 1877.

succession, the last crop of kidney beans, and a few of the turnip-rooted kind of radish. Stake scarlet beans. The main plantations of borecoles must now be

JULY

1594   A licence was granted to John Pedler, a blind Exbourne harper, to beg in parts of Devon.

1836   A dozen London policemen visited Okehampton in their black velvet shooting-jackets and 'finer-looking better-behaved men could not have been selected'.

1857   Mark Corner, labourer, was sentenced to one month's imprisonment at hard labour for riding through Culmstock village in a wagon drawn by a horse without reins and giving his name to a constable as 'Tom Bird'.

1889   It was announced that St Sidwell's Church was to be lit by electricity.

❧ 10 ❧

1604   Twenty-one buildings were destroyed by a great fire in Ottery St Mary leaving more than 130 persons homeless.

1688   Mary Southmead of Alphington was convicted of stealing raspberries and ordered to be fined or whipped.

1824   Joseph King, 'a man of colour whose face was curiously tattooed', was convicted at Exeter of stealing four pocket handkerchiefs and sentenced to one month's imprisonment at hard labour.

1858   Joseph Stamp, Exeter shopkeeper, was fined for selling sweet-meats on Sunday.

❧ 11 ❧

1510   The city of Exeter decided that each parish shall celebrate only the church holy days and not the revels by 'the young men...called Robin Hood'.

made. This is the month for planting the principal crops of winter greens. Thin out annuals during showery weather. ❀ 1898 – *In the first week sow peas for*

JULY

1771 James Cook was off Start Point in the *Endeavour* returning from Tahiti.

1792 Mr O'Brien, the Irish Giant, was on show in Exeter and reputedly stood nearly nine feet high.

1936 It was reported that electricity would soon be available at Morchard Bishop.

❧ 12 ❧

Birthday of Bampfylde-Moore Carew, King of the Gypsies, also known as King of the Beggars: born at Bickleigh, 1690

Birthday of Charles Kingsley, author of *Westward Ho !*: born at Holne, 1819

1610 Richard Wilkins was executed at Exeter for the crime of witchcraft.

1622 Walter Yonge of Colyton wrote 'there was a great fish came ashore at Seaton, which was 23 feet and 3 inches in length. The fork of his tail, from end to end, was 5 foot 1 inch and ½ inch over. The compass about the middle of the fish was 9 foot and 9 inches. The said fish had no gills but put out his water at his pole. His fins were like leather which keeps the dirt from a coach wheel, without any gristles. His skin very smooth as an eel but exceeding black, except under the belly, which was as white. His tail stood not as other fishes, at the ridge bone of his back, but from side to side. He had not any scales. His teeth were big, round and sharp. His flesh was very white and felt like fat of pork'.

1771 A yacht built in Topsham, 27 feet long with a main sail, fore sail, 2 jibs and top sail was for sale.

1776 Captain James Cook left Plymouth in the *Resolution* intending to sail around North America by the Pacific.

the last crop of the season. In the last week sow yellow turnips for a full winter crop, and spinach for an early winter supply. Gather and dry medicinal and

JULY

❧ 13 ❧

1561 The grammar school at Plymouth was established with the appointment of Thomas Brooke to teach 'all the children native and inhabitant within the town'.

1597 Richard Hawkes of Rewe was granted a licence to transport butter, cheese and grain from Somerset and Dorset into Devon.

1767 William Lee and Margaret Symons were transported from Exeter for stealing geese.

1829 Twenty varieties of strawberry were grown in one Monkleigh garden.

❧ 14 ❧

1636 For the second year the justices at Exeter ordered restrictions on selling barley.

1877 A public meeting for the Sunday closure of public houses was held in Exeter.

1881 A Plymouth policeman was given 2 guineas by the Bathing Association for saving the life of a young woman swimming off the Hoe.

❧ 15 ❧
St Swithins Day

1726 North Sea codfish was on sale at Exeter's quay.

1752 Rain at Lympstone, it was claimed, 'adds to the superstition of the people'.

potherbs; also propagate such by slips and cuttings. Continue the summer pruning and training of all wall trees. Take up the remainder of tuberous roots, such as

JULY

1858 The annual school treat at Cullompton took place in the grounds of the vicarage. Prior to the tea there was a procession headed by the Town Band and afterwards various amusements took place including a dance in the evening 'enjoyed by the young folks of the town who were permitted to amuse themselves on the lawn'.

1950 Winston Churchill gave a speech at Saltram.

❧ 16 ❧

Birthday of Sir Joshua Reynolds, Devon portrait painter: born at Plympton, 1723.

1452 Henry VI visited Ottery St Mary.

1590 Richard Ferris, continuing his voyage in a wherry around the South West, left Ilton Castle near Salcombe and sailed to Plymouth where he had 'great entertainment' on a naval ship.

1622 Dodbrooke's rector claimed he was slandered by John Maskell calling him a knave, an arrant knave, a very knave, a dissembling knave and a 'sh*t-breech knave'.

1827 Abraham Cann won first prize of twenty pounds in the Totnes Wrestling Match.

❧ 17 ❧

1452 Henry VI began a visit to Exeter.

1635 Thomasine Bovey, a widow from Totnes, gave her daughter Agnes, 'a little maid', as apprentice to Anthony and Dorothy Jarvis of Ide, 'honest people as I so trust'.

anemone, ranunculus, etc. ✺ 1900 – *Some of the cabbages sown in May may now be planted for autumn and early winter use. The main crop of celery*

JULY

1671 King Charles II, and his brother James, Duke of York, visited Plymouth.

1671 The clerk of Holcombe Burnell was accused of swearing and cursing.

1770 Jerkin, Oberon and Whirligig were entered for the first day of racing at Haldon.

1854 A flock of forty Turtle Doves was seen at Dawlish Warren.

❧ 18 ❧

1622 Henry Wallis was accused of slandering John Browne of Upottery by calling him a whoremonger who 'keeps a whore in every bush'.

1671 Charles II touched 18 persons for the King's Evil in Plymouth.

1805 A site was chosen for the 3war prison on Dartmoor.

1822 A man pulled a large cartwheel from Moretonhampstead to Exeter in two hours and 29 minutes for a wager of 25 shillings.

1897 In honour of Queen Victoria's 60th anniversary a pear was grafted onto a thornbush at Sunnyland in Ottery St Mary.

1927 An afternoon hailstorm caused considerable damage in North Devon including breaking more than 500 panes of glass in Hartland.

❧ 19 ❧

Armada Day (Plymouth)

1727 An earthquake was reported in Exeter.

should be planted the first favourable weather. Sow in the first week the last crop of kidney beans. Scarlet runners will now require staking. Cherries, peaches or

JULY

1825 Recorded as the hottest day then known in Barnstaple.

1832 A visitor newly arrived from London was the first cholera case in Exeter.

1852 Queen Victoria visited Babbacombe.

1889 Progress was announced on erecting a monument to the Prince of Orange at Brixham.

❧ 20 ❧

1588 After years of anticipation the Spanish Armada was sighted off Plymouth.

1822 The Reverend Daniel Lysons dedicated his great history of Devon.

1831 Monsieur P. Daguiere & Company's Grand Peristrephic or Moving Panorama of the French Revolution of 1831 was on view in Exeter.

1832 The second reported cholera case in Exeter was a woman newly arrived from Plymouth who died the next day.

1852 Paignton won a cricket match against South Devon.

❧ 21 ❧

1644 Princess Henrietta Maria, daughter of Charles I and Henrietta Maria, was baptised in Exeter Cathedral.

1668 Francis Hanne of Loxbeare admitted spending an evening at a Tiverton alehouse but claimed he was with a woman solely to discuss the waywardness of another parishioner, acknowledged drinking cider 'for the satisfying of nature' but was ignorant as to the vomit found in his room.

plums may now be budded. Annuals may be thinned out in showery weather. Layer carnations towards the middle or end of the month. ✻ *1901 – Earth up*

JULY

1823 Wrestling and 'rustic sports' took place on the Hoe in Plymouth.

1881 In a garden in Bull Point, Plymouth, 'monster' gooseberries (reportedly larger than plums) were picked.

1939 A Chagford parish meeting discussed communal billeting of child evacuees in the event of war.

❧ 22 ❦

1676 At midnight the newly-built *Expedition* of Plymouth caught fire while at anchor in Catwater.

1767 Princess Amelia arrived in Exeter en route for Plymouth.

1824 At midnight Mr G-s and Miss F-d eloped from Dartmouth in a coach and four.

1864 It was reported that as many as 500 people were using the public bathing place near Head Weir in Exeter and as yet no improper language had been overheard.

1939 The Royal family visited the Royal Naval College at Dartmouth.

❧ 23 ❦

1389 Permission was granted to cut down two trees in Exeter's Cathedral Yard.

1596 A pair of twin boys were baptised and buried in Barnstaple.

1602 The *Concord* returned to Exmouth from one of the first English voyages to New England.

1767 Princess Amelia visited Mount Edgcumbe.

and stick peas, and earth up and top advancing beans. Plant the main crop of celery the first suitable weather. Sow lettuce for succession, the last crop of kidney

JULY

1827 Torrington had a Gala Day with the limekilns being lit on the canal.

1832 Cholera deaths continued at Exeter.

1903 The Prince and Princess of Wales launched the *King Edward VII* at Plymouth.

❧ 24 ❧

Astrological Sign of LEO, the Lion
(until August 23rd)

1661 Richard Alford of Escot testified that a preacher was found 'preaching, as he calleth it, unto a great number of people called Quakers, and met together contrary to law in one Glanfeeld's house where I heard him utter many expressions that tend to sedition'.

1854 Lightning killed many sheep at Heavitree.

1857 The Exeter Coroner held an inquest at the Red Cow Inn into the death of Susan Tothill, a sixty-year-old woman resident in Cheriton Fitzpaine. A local surgeon gave evidence that her death was caused by 'rapid walking'.

1870 The hottest day of the year in Jacobstowe at 82°.

❧ 25 ❧

1603 A hogshead of beer and a barrel of gunpowder was purchased by Plymouth Corporation to mark the Coronation of James I.

1764 Six Topsham houses were destroyed by fire.

1771 One thousand salmon were reportedly caught in the last week between Exeter and Topsham.

beans, and a few of the turnip-rooted kind of radish. Stake scarlet beans. The main plantations of borecoles must now be made. This is the month for planting

JULY

1809 Quicksilver beat White Rose in Totnes Races for the £50 plate.

1857 It was reported in *Woolmer's Exeter and Plymouth Gazette* that the 'quiet nook' of Kingsteignton was disturbed by a fracas between the vicar and an 'emissary of the Latter-Day Saints' who came to 'harangue' the villagers showing his 'great ignorance of the English language, fearful perversions of holy writ, and most extravagant assumptions of miraculous powers'.

1939 A flitch of bacon was given at the Halwill village fete to the couple who demonstrated the most matrimonial happiness in a year and one day.

❧ 26 ❧

1584 Sir Walter Raleigh asked to purchase Hayes Barton from the current owner and wrote of the 'natural disposition I have to that place having been born in that house'.

1690 The French plundered and burned Teignmouth.

1815 Great interest greeted Napoleon Bonaparte's arrival in Plymouth Harbour on the *Bellerophon* en route to St Helena.

1823 It was reported from Plymouth that a young woman died as a result of efforts to reduce her waist from 'tight lacing'.

1831 An Exeter woman 'of easy virtue' was exhibited in the stocks for two hours.

1944 *Snow White and the Seven Dwarfs* played at the Gaumont in Exeter.

the principal crops of winter greens. Thin out annuals during showery weather. ❋ *1907 – During this month prepare all unoccupied lots of ground*

JULY

❧ 27 ❧

1649 John Taylor, the poet, walked from Exeter to Honiton where he stayed the night and wrote he had 'a diet of such a homely fashion as I have no occasion to boast of'.

1821 Fire destroyed a cottage in Sampford Peverell.

1877 It was reported that the Topsham and District Horticultural and Cottage Garden Society's exhibition was held at The Retreat and a prize was given for 'best specimen of pillow lace the work of the daughters of cottagers in the district'.

1883 Edmond's (formerly Wombwell's) Royal Windsor Castle Menagerie processed up Fore Street in Exeter from Starcross.

❧ 28 ❧

1658 Sir Courtenay Pole left East London with the corpse of his father for Colyton.

1858 It was reported that a 'reverend ruffian' had left Plymouth after fathering the child of a seventeen-year old girl.

1881 The temperature fell to 41° in Babbacombe.

1882 The Torquay Choral Society's open air concert was held at Watcombe.

1883 Residents in an Exeter suburb were surprised to see a man in *puris naturalibis* walking briskly in the morning. The man was returned to his attendants from whom he had just escaped.

1911 The competitors in the *Daily Mail* Circuit of Great Britain landed at Exeter.

for autumn and winter crops. Continue sowing radishes, lettuces, and turnips.
Plant out broccoli, savoys, leeks, cauliflowers, and winter cabbages, and earth

117]

JULY

❧ 29 ❧

1669   East Buckland's vicar accused Thomasine Downe of leading an immoral life in keeping 'company with her husband's brother in a very suspicious manner', being found lying with him in a ditch and having 'a very lewd and wicked life and conversation and hath divers times or at least once offered to prostitute her body to commit adultery or uncleanliness'. She claimed he had 'attempted her chastity and did endeavour to force her'.

1670   Mary, wife of Will Hooper, 'killed herself in ripping open her belly and tearing her guts in pieces'.

1782   At Heavitree Rebecca Downing was burnt at the stake for poisoning her master.

1827   A great thunderstorm hit Exeter from 8 to 11 p.m.

1864   Mr Simms and his Marionettes performed to crowded audiences in Honiton.

1870   It was reported in *The Devon Weekly Times* that Mr Murch of Broadgate in Exeter was the sole agent in the city for American Iced Cream Soda which was recommended as a 'delightfully cool and refreshing' beverage.

❧ 30 ❧

1427   Thomas Buk of Dartmouth robbed a Scottish vessel near the French port of Oleron.

1569   The travelling company of the Earl of Leicester played at Dartmouth.

1653   Barnstaple's Tomb Stone, on which merchants struck deals, was re-erected on the quay.

up celery. Divest wall trees of all superfluous shoots. Continue to water in dry weather both morning and evening, and gather all sorts of seeds as they advance

JULY

1883 At Exeter visitors flocked to see Edmond's Royal Windsor Castle Menagerie including the leopards, camels, wolves, snakes, monkeys, kangaroos, raccoons, gnus, bears, elephants, rhinoceros, tigers, zebras and Wallace the lion.

1928 A procession preceded a meeting at Exeter of the League of Nations Union.

❧ 31 ❦

1675 The haymakers at Sydenham were paid one pound and eight shillings (in total) for their labour.

1827 Mr Sams of Bath advertised his service at Plymouth in the curing of stammering.

1857 Among the prizes awarded by the Devon and Exeter Botanical and Horticultural Society's Exhibition were to Lady Rolle for her collection of pineapples and to J.W. Buller for 'Best new plant, of any description, in bloom, never before exhibited for a prize at the society's exhibition'.

1948 Tourism was expected to be boosted by knitted bathing costumes being released from coupons.

to maturity. Propagate roses and other shrubs by laying the young wood. Bud roses in cloudy weather, and divide the roots of double primroses and auriculas. ❁❁

AUGUST

Dry August and warm,
Doth harvest no harm.

Thomas Tusser, 1557

AUGUST

❧ 1 ❦

Lammas Day. Exeter Lammas Fair

1636 Margaret Snelling was convicted of 'deceiving and cosening of the King's subjects by fortune telling and deluding them' and ordered to be publicly whipped and pilloried at the next market day in Exeter.

1725 The Red Lion Inn at Exeter was reopened.

1792 It was urged in Exeter that fruit-women should not sell unripe fruit to children because it was poisonous.

1859 To celebrate the opening of the railway line to Paignton a special Paignton Pudding, weighing 1½ tons, was paraded through the streets in a wagon drawn by eight horses.

1870 The workers of Mr W. Adams, Crediton shoe manufacturer, had a day's outing by rail to Teignmouth and dined at the Devon Arms.

1901 Arthur Conan Doyle's *The Hound of the Baskervilles* was published in *The Strand Magazine*.

❧ 2 ❦

1282 William Coffin won a legal case regarding 500 acres of grazing rights in Lynton.

1831 The release was reported in *The Western Luminary* of Aaron Rutley, 21, and Robert Allan, 22, who were charged with stealing an umbrella at Cullompton.

1879 Thunderstorms caused damage to Devon ships and crops.

1883 Brilliant sunshine and drying winds reduced complaints of hay fever in Bradford which made one remedy ('have your

✸✸✸ 1891 – *Sow German greens, parsley, savoys, early cabbages, and onions, for the succeeding year, and spinach, lettuces and cauliflowers, to stand the*

AUGUST

head shaved and a mustard poultice put on to draw the nonsense out') superfluous.

❧ 3 ❧

1624 John Stricke, son of Thomas Stricke of Parkham, admitted stealing money because he was hungry, paying six pence for a few handfuls of nuts and then leaving to play with other boys.

1857 The new Public Baths were opened in Torquay.

1876 The Horse, Donkey, Dog and Flower Show was held at Bideford and Lady Jane won first prize as best donkey.

1883 It was reported in Exeter that the late Lord Rolle's will forbid any trees to be cut down within two miles of Bicton House.

❧ 4 ❧

1549 A riot broke out in Exeter in support of the Prayer Book Rebels encamped outside the gates. The rioters cried out 'Come out these heretics and twopenny bookmen! Where be they? By God's wounds and blood, we will not be pinned in to serve their turns: we will go out and have in our neighbours; they be honest, good and godly men'.

1651 Mary Thorne of Exeter overheard John Hayne say regarding a rumour of Royalists taking over the city 'Major Saunders was a black-livered rogue and wondered with what face the brune-faced toad would look them in the face when they should come'.

1870 Nearly four inches of rain fell at Zeal Monachorum.

winter. ❀ 1896 – *Sow a few early horn carrots, and at the close of the month the main crop of winter spinach. About the end of the second week sow lettuce for*

AUGUST

❧ 5 ❧

1612 **T**iverton suffered devastation by fire – only fourteen years after the first major fire.

1832 **A** sixteen-foot long white whale was spotted off Berry Head.

1914 **O**ne of the first Plymouth casualties of the war was HMS *Amphion* which hit a mine and sunk.

❧ 6 ❧

1549 **L**ord Russell, with the Royal infantry as well as Italian and German soldiers, entered Exeter at eight o'clock in the morning and ended the siege of the Prayer Book Rebellion.

1550 **J**esus Day. A sermon was preached in the Cathedral to mark the end of the Prayer Book Rebellion.

1779 **A** French fleet of some 66 vessels anchored off Plymouth Sound with the intent of burning Plymouth Dock.

1792 **T**he birthday of Lord Courtenay was celebrated at Powderham Castle by more than 300 guests at a masquerade ball among whom were present a Highland Chief, Tippoo Saih and 2 sons as hostage prisoners, two Cherokee chiefs 'with their squaws', a Quaker, The Gigantic Door-Keeper, Nuns, Friars, Old Women Ballad-singers, Fruit and Flower Girls, Shepherds, Shepherdesses and Devonshire Farmers.

❧ 7 ❧

1582 **L**ady Elizabeth Russell, daughter of Francis second earl of Bedford, was married to William, third earl of Bath, in Exeter followed by a 'triumph' in Southernhay, a wedding feast at

standing through the winter. Earth up the earliest celery. Plant out the last crop of broccoli. Protect ripe fruit from wasps and insects. Remove all useless growths

AUGUST

Bedford House and the city presenting the couple with a ewer and basin of silver gilt.

1770 Mary Quaram of Newton Bushel was sentenced to death for drowning her grandson.

1821 The Reverend George Oliver's *History of Exeter* was published.

1829 In Exeter a cow knocked down the glass and china stall belonging to Mr Bull.

1939 The Mayor and Mayoress of Barnstaple met the Mayor of New York before travelling to Barnstable, Massachusetts, for that town's Tercentennary celebrations.

❧ 8 ❦

1771 A surplus of herrings caught between Teignmouth and Dawlish resulted in their being buried in the sands.

1851 A Plymouth trawlerman hauled nets and found the body of his father, who unknowingly to his son, had drowned earlier that day.

1871 (8th–10th) Falling stars were seen in Zeal Monachorum.

1881 The two-oared race (for women only) at the Totnes & Bridgetown Regatta was won by *The Comet* of the Kingsbridge Rowing Club.

❧ 9 ❦

1678 William Gould the rector of Kenn was called debauched, wicked and obscene and accused of visiting 'very suspected houses' in Exeter, going to an Ottery St Mary alehouse, and at Honiton visiting 'Joan the whore'.

from vines. Remove annuals as soon as their flowers decay. Cut down raspberry canes which have ripened off their fruit. ✱ *1898 – Sow winter and spring*

AUGUST

1822 The first man to sound the new bell in Kentisbeare church reportedly dropped dead within the minute.

1852 The *Mosquito* won First Prize of the Torquay Regatta.

1881 The Lawn Tennis Tournament finished in Exmouth.

1883 Inmates of the Exeter Workhouse had an outing to Woodbury Common where they enjoyed buns, ginger beer, tea and tobacco as well as cricket, dancing and Aunt Sally.

❧ 10 ❦

1287 One thousand tiles were purchased for Exeter Cathedral.

1389 The *George* was loaded at Dartmouth with cloth for Spain.

1831 William Atkins, 23, Joseph Stocker, 16, and Henry Pearse, 16, were committed to the county gaol on a charge of wilful murder regarding an incident in the Tom & Jerry beer shop in Broadclyst.

1838 A squirrel with a white tail was seen in Yealmpton.

1852 Emigrants for Australia, who were about to board the *Dinapore* at Dartmouth, visited Totnes and were reported as 'appearing respectable people'.

1883 A tug of war was held in Holsworthy between Royal Engineers and the Navy.

1948 HMS *Valiant* left Plymouth for the Clyde to be broken up.

❧ 11 ❦

1657 A brick partition was to be erected in the Cathedral, in order to have several congregations share the building, at a cost of £150.

spinach in the beginning and about the end of the month; parsley and winter onions, for a full crop, in the first week; cabbages, cauliflowers, savoys, and

AUGUST

1890   Festival of the East Budleigh branch of the Rational Sick and Burial Association.

1917   At Okehampton a garden party was given to Devonians wounded in the war.

1973   A Wreck fish was caught off the Eddystone.

❧ 12 ❧

1654   Diana Crosse, an Exeter widow, was accused of witchcraft. Mr Ezekiel Trible, a tobacco pipe maker, alleged that she caused his pipes not to work properly.

1657   The Deputy Recorder of Barnstaple was dismissed for 'imbecility of mind and body, and age'.

1746   The Reverend Charles Wesley preached at Tavistock.

1812   The foundation stone of Plymouth Breakwater was laid.

1940   A woman was killed in a bombing raid on Plymouth.

❧ 13 ❧

1735   The curate of Georgeham was found guilty of drunkenness.

1752   Baptism at Ashburton of John Tripe, later known as John Swete, author of *The Picturesque Sketches of Devon*.

1765   There were rumours in South Molton of civil unrest due to high grain prices.

1792   Death of Thomas Whittey, manufacturer of Axminster Carpets.

1871   Thunderstorms hit Dartmoor, Ashburton and Plymouth.

German greens about the middle of the month, for planting out in spring; lettuce in the first and last weeks. Examine bulbs that are out of the

AUGUST

1889 A Bee-eater was seen in Stoke Wood near Exeter.

1936 The Victorian cygnet boat was relaunched at Starcross.

❧ 14 ❧

1159 An agreement was reached between the Earl of Devon and the Bishop of Exeter over the rights of Tiverton's church.

1682 Temperance Lloyd, Mary Trembles and Susannah Edwards were convicted of witchcraft and sentenced to death at Exeter.

1862 The first meeting of the Devonshire Association was held in Exeter.

1883 The apricot harvest reportedly failed at Powderham Castle but a large crop of apples (including Keswick Castle, Lemon Pippin, King of the Pippins, Winter Greening) was expected.

1917 A thunderstorm caused massive flooding across Dartmoor.

❧ 15 ❧

1827 Pavilion beat Gypsey for the purse of 40 sovereigns at Honiton Races and three gypsies were arrested for swindling.

1851 At Exeter Patrick Crawley was convicted of playing pitch and toss in Cathedral Yard and ordered to either pay a fine of 5 shillings or be locked in a dark cell for one day.

1931 The last electric tram ran in Exeter.

1952 (15th–16th) Heavy rain caused a destructive flood at Lynmouth with a severe loss in lives and property.

---

ground. ❋ *1900 – Earth up and top beans when in full bloom. Hoe between all advancing crops of greens. Early in the month prepare in an open spot a bed*

AUGUST

❧ 16 ❧

1676 Fire swept through North Tawton.

1792 Three men competed to catch one particular salmon at Axminster and one of the men, George Love, drowned.

1831 It was reported that the *Falcon* won the Silver Cup at the Teignmouth Regatta and that the rowing match was 'well contested' by the Starcross Lumper crews of the *Ariel*, *Red Rover* and *Induction*.

❧ 17 ❧

1387 John Sparke of Exeter was granted permission to travel to Rome.

1767 A brawl broke out between Tiverton's capital burgesses.

1820 Diana beat Gypsy and Black Sally in the Salcombe and Sidmouth Races.

1857 James Brookes of Exeter was remanded on the charge of stealing apples.

1877 On the German training corvette *Niobe* in Dartmouth was Prince Henry, eldest son of the Crown Prince of Germany and a grandson of Victoria.

❧ 18 ❧

1821 News reached Plymouth that labourers and mechanics in the Dockyard would work only from Monday to Friday.

1880 Thousands of spectators on the Hoe watched the Plymouth Swimming Matches.

1910 The Empire Electric Theatre opened in Exeter.

for sowing cabbages for the main spring or early summer supply. Earth up the earliest celery. Protect cucumbers from heavy rains. Sow lettuce for standing

AUGUST

❧ 19 ❦

1821 A sermon on the death of Queen Charlotte was given in Sidmouth.

1852 A lightning bolt struck the double locks house near Exeter and killed one of the two men inside.

1857 The Tamar Archery Meeting was held in the presence of the Duke and Duchess of Northumberland.

1870 The potato crop in Bideford was reported to have less disease than known previously.

❧ 20 ❦

1566 John Walsh admitted to the bishop's official that there were three kinds of fairies (white, green and black fairies which were the worst) and that he met them on hills at midday.

1827 Five very large gooseberries, one measuring 4½ inches, were grown in St David's parish near Exeter.

1832 Two cholera deaths were reported in a lodging house in Honiton while in Plymouth there were 547 deaths since early June.

1920 An editorial in *The Western Times* supported the establishment of a commercial motor road transport system while in Clovelly, for the first time, a motor car drove up and down the cobbled High Street.

❧ 21 ❦

Birthday of Andrew Brice, pre-eminent printer: born at Exeter, 1692.

through the winter. Make new plantations of strawberries. Pot auriculas. Take up bulbs. Layer carnations. ❋ 1901 – *Sow a few early horn carrots, and at the*

AUGUST

1765   Fire swept through Honiton.

1779   A storm drove the French fleet, then blockading Plymouth, from their safe anchorage and by the English navy back to France.

1840-1845   Speech Day at Blundell's School, Tiverton.

1876   At Barnstaple a nightly stench was reportedly as strong as ever.

❧ 22 ❧

Birthday of William Hayman Cummings, musician, adapter of 'Hark! the Herald Angels Sing': born at Sidbury, 1831

1771   Lord Chatham was given the freedom of the city of Exeter.

1807   The foundation stone of the Devon County House of Correction was laid.

1829   Ten wild ducks seen flying over Barnstaple were responsible for predictions of stormy and unseasonable weather.

1831   At the Starcross Regatta the *Falcon* of Torquay won the Powderham Cup and the prize for six oared boats was won by the *Red Rover* of Exeter.

1835   It was reported that on the coach from Tavistock to Plymouth a woman's dress caught fire from a fellow passenger's cigar.

❧ 23 ❧

1537   Henry VIII gave the city of Exeter the status of a county.

1596   Leonard Calbone was murdered outside Exeter's South Gate by a fellow soldier.

close of the month the main crop of winter spinach. About the end of the second week sow lettuce for standing through the winter. Earth up the earliest celery.

AUGUST

1792 A young Barnstaple man sought to escape his relations by shooting himself at South Molton.

1822 A sparrow was chased into an Exeter house by a hawk and both birds were caught by the owner.

❧ 24 ❧

Astrological Sign of VIRGO, the Virgin
(through to September 23rd)

1591 Baptism in London of Robert Herrick, author of *Hesperides* and incumbent of Dean Prior from 1629 to 1647 and 1662 to 1674. His writings have earned him a reputation for disliking Devon.

1821 Marriage at Plympton St Mary of Richard Lapthorne to Mary Ford who had been married four times previously, all in the same church where each husband was subsequently buried.

1866 A waterspout was seen at Meshaw.

1870 Prizes were given for Women's Work in the Poltimore Cottage Garden Exhibition for best specimen of needlework in garment, best made stout shirt and best pair of knitted man's stockings.

1945 The first batch of temporary council houses in Rifford Road, Exeter, was reported as nearly ready for occupancy.

❧ 25 ❧

1676 At Sydenham the otter hunters were given five shillings for their efforts.

1792 A Paignton smuggler was wrecked at Dartmouth.

Plant out the last crop of broccoli. Protect ripe fruit from wasps and insects. Remove all useless growths from vines. Remove annuals as soon as their flowers

AUGUST

1882 At a harvest supper in Pudddington one old man lamented the coming of machine threshing machines and claimed 'men were men afore the reaping machines came up, but now there isn't one of them worth a darned nought for a day's work now'.

1917 An earthquake shook Princetown.

1950 Devonport-manned aircraft carrier *Unicorn* left Hong Kong for service in Korea.

❧ 26 ❧

1658 Nearly 100 persons rioted when Exeter's mayor ordered the bells of St John's church to be removed: workmen were pelted with dirt and stones and called thieves and church robbers.

1768 James Cook sailed from Plymouth in the *Endeavour* for Tahiti.

1831 Opening of the Floating Bridge across the river Dart at Dartmouth.

1864 A Silverton hunter set off for hares and by mistake killed 'Shot', his favourite spaniel.

1940 Bombs fell throughout Plymouth.

❧ 27 ❧

1741 The foundation stone of the Devon & Exeter Hospital was laid.

1831 A steamer loaded with sheep left Topsham for London where it was said Devonshire mutton was highly prized.

1889 Among the wedding presents received by a pair of Sidmouth

decay. Cut down raspberry canes which have ripened off their fruit.
❁ *1907 – Sow German greens, parsley, savoys, early cabbages and onions, for*

133]

AUGUST

newlyweds were a lizard skin handbag, a gong mounted with horns, a crumb scoop, four silver fern pots and *Essays on Criticism*.

❧ 28 ❧

1688 Over £52 worth of spring bulbs were purchased for the garden at Forde in Newton Abbot.

1764 A reunion was held in Crediton of five brothers last together sometime before 1734.

1880 The harvest was completed at Babbacombe.

1889 A false alarm was sounded at Sidmouth when a steam collier was mistaken for an enemy gunboat.

1976 The last day of five weeks of unbroken sunny weather.

❧ 29 ❧

1653 Thomas Heard was buried. Nothing more has been written about him, nor probably ever will, unless a family historian discovers a connection. Like many hundreds of thousands of other Devonians before and since the course of his life, his dreams, hopes, frustrations, joys and sorrows, lie forgotten in a grass-covered grave.

1767 Workmen digging in St Sidwell's parish found ancient coins.

1789 The Reverend John Wesley preached at Tavistock and Plymouth Dock.

1792 It was reported that several factory owners were given children from the Exeter Workhouse.

the succeeding year, and spinach, lettuces, and cauliflowers to stand the winter. Earth up celery; hoe and transplant cauliflowers, savoys, and broccoli, and the

AUGUST

❧ 30 ❧

1798 There was anxiety at Saltram regarding the replacement of the head gardener.

1882 There was speculation over what the Dean of Exeter Cathedral uttered when he broke his leg on holiday.

1889 A young lad of Exeter was fined five shillings for unlawfully and cruelly torturing and ill-treating a cat.

1937 The Odeon Cinema opened in Exeter featuring *The Charge of the Light Brigade* with Errol Flynn and Olivia De Havilland.

❧ 31 ❧

1591 Battle of Sir Richard Grenville of the *Revenge* with the Spanish fleet. Grenville was carried to a Spanish vessel.

1835 Fire destroyed Fanny Bennet's house in Abbotsham because of her attempts to disperse a strange swarm of bees with a torch.

1881 Madame Gent gave several examples of natation at the Devonport Swimming Matches held off Mount Wise.

main crop of celery intro trenches for blanching. Cut those herbs which are adapted for distillation. Take up garlic, that is withered in the stem. ✺✺✺

"FOR THE BLOOD IS THE LIFE."

CLARKE'S
WORLD FAMED
BLOOD MIXTURE.

THE GREAT BLOOD PURIFIER AND RESTORER.

Largest sale of any Medicine in the World.

For cleansing and clearing the blood from all impurities, cannot be too highly recommended. For Scrofula, Scurvy, Skin and Blood Diseases, and Sores of all kinds, it is a never-failing and permanent cure.

It Cures Old Sores
Cures Ulcerated Sore Legs
Cures Scurvy Sores
Cures Cancerous Ulcers
Cures Glandular Swellings
Cures Blackheads, or Pimples on the Face
Cures Blood and Skin Diseases
Cures Ulcerated Sores on the Neck

Clears the Blood from all impure matter, from whatever cause arising.

As this mixture is pleasant to the taste, and warranted free from anything injurious to the most delicate constitution of either sex, the Proprietor solicits sufferers to give it trial to test its value.

Thousands of Testimonials from all parts of the World.

Cure of a Bad Ulcerated Foot:

" North-street, Audenshaw (near Manchester,) January 10th, 1882."

" It affords me great pleasure to add my testimony to the wonderful effects of your Blood Mixture, which has cured me of a very bad ulcerated foot and ankle. I had four wounds, which prevented me following my occupation for four years, during which time I have been in five different infirmaries and under fifteen different doctors. I was at last induced to try your Blood Mixture, and after taken three small bottles I was able to go to work, and by the time I had taken nine or ten bottles I was completely cured. Make whatever use you like of this, for the benefit of other sufferers.—I am yours respectfully.

"JOHN WILLIAMS."

Cure of Abscesses.

" Harlow, Essex, February 23rd, 1880."

" I was laid up for four years and a half, not able to do anything, with abscesses on my body. I tried four medical men, and found no benefit from their treatment. I was then sent as an in-patient to a London hospital with a similar result. Being discharged from there, I was recommended to try your ' Blood Mixture,' and after taking two 11s. bottles (bought from Mr. Campion, Chemist, here) I was able to return to my work, and have continued well ever since. Accept my grateful thanks.—Yours truly.

"GEORGE JUDD."

How to Save Coals.

Slow Combustion Cooking Stoves.

BURN HALF THE AMOUNT OF COAL

THAT THE ORDINARY STOVES DO.

Slow Combustion Warming Stoves.*

Testimonials of these Stoves that have been in Use for 50 and 40 Years, and particulars of

HEARDER & SON,

General Manufacturers
195
UNION STREET,
PLYMOUTH.

ESTABLISHED 1770.

CAUTION.—Messrs. H. & SON feel sorry to be obliged to caution the public against spurious imitations of these world-renowned Stoves. They can only be obtained of the Inventors, at their Manufactory, 195 Union Street, Plymouth.

* For Halls, Shops, Churches, Schools, Harness, or Drawing Rooms, on Dr. HEARDER'S Improved "Arnott" Principle.

DEVONPORT
ROYAL HOTEL.

This Hotel is close to the Dock-yard, Government Offices, and Terminus of the London & South Western Railway Station.

J. E. PARKER, MANAGER.

TABLE D'HOTE DAILY AT 7 P.M.

SEPTEMBER

September blow soft,
Till fruit be in loft.

Thomas Tusser, 1557

SEPTEMBER

❧ 1 ❧

1880 There was a 'Sham Fight' in the Brickfields at Plymouth.

1882 Farmers claimed that foxes were so numerous in Holsworthy that it was not worth preserving them just for the Hunt's chase.

1945 The Yankee Doodle Circus came to Exeter Haven Banks.

❧ 2 ❧

1651 Bags of wool imported to Barnstaple were 'opened and sufficiently aired' because of fears of plague.

1765 There were Italian fireworks set off in Cathedral Close in Exeter.

1829 An 'Ethiopian-complexioned gentleman alias a purifier of chimneys' was fined five shillings for 'Bacchanalian irregularity' at Exeter.

1851 The *Volante* won the Challenge Cup at the Teignmouth Regatta.

1879 Nine convicts tried to escape from Dartmoor Prison while making hay.

1879 A lad of thirteen was pushed over the quay at Torquay in a public crush to see the Prince of Wales and later died.

1880 Cetewayo, King of the Zulus, arrived in Plymouth on the *Nubian*.

1882 Mr S.C. Hall gave a talk for 2½ hours, without notes, at the Plymouth Free Public Library where he had bequeathed his books.

❋❋❋ 1891 ❋ *Sow vegetable seeds for a spring crop, and plant German greens.*
❋ 1896 – *Take up potatoes as soon as they are ripe. Plant out coleworts. Plant*

[138

SEPTEMBER

❧ 3 ❧

1389 Richard II pardoned the Bishop for allowing felons and convicted clerics to escape from their imprisonment.

1675 Two Plymouth servants were reported to have poisoned their mistress by putting 'mercury into her broth and after she had eaten a little, she found herself sick. She leaving the broth her husband ate some of it, which also made him sick, after which their daughter took up more broth to what they left and ate it all up. They were poisoned and the next day the woman of the house died, since which the daughter is dead and the old man is very ill and supposed not to recover'.

1752 (3rd–13th) Nothing happened in Devon except the date changed.

1832 A rock melon, weighing fourteen pounds, was picked in a Heavitree garden.

❧ 4 ❧

1633 Exmouth's ferry boat sank and three men drowned.

1789 The Reverend John Swete left his Kenton home for the first tour of his *Picturesque Sketches of Devon*.

1879 The wrestling at Commercial Road in Exeter was reported to be 'of a first-class order'.

1920 (4th–14th) At Plymouth Tercentenary Celebrations began of the voyage of the *Mayflower* to America.

❧ 5 ❧

1643 Articles of surrender were signed and the Royalists took control of Exeter ending a year of pro-Parliamentarian rule.

out lettuces to stand till winter in sheltered situations. Gather any apples or pears which may ripen this month. Various hardy annuals if sown now will

SEPTEMBER

The defenders endured the jeers of the soldiers of Prince Maurice:

> *Where is your God now, O ye hypocrites?*
> *Where is your holy cause, your cause and all your hopes?*

1879 A public meeting in Crediton welcomed home two soldiers fighting in the Zulu War.

1881 Kingsteignton's heaviest recorded fall of rain of 2.43 inches.

1883 Complaints were made of the excessive odours near Exmouth's railway station.

1887 Disaster struck on the first night of *The Romany Rye* at Exeter's Theatre Royal: more than 160 persons lost their lives in a fire which consumed the theatre.

❧ 6 ☙

1620 The *Mayflower* left Plymouth for America.

1792 The first part of the Reverend Polwhele's *History of Devonshire* was advertised for sale by subscription.

1824 Mr Graham began filling his great balloon with gas in Cathedral Yard in Exeter.

❧ 7 ☙

1774 The Reverend John Wesley preached at Tavistock.

1824 A large crowd gathered in Exeter to watch Mr Graham ascend in his balloon and at about four in the afternoon it rose and floated West by North West. Nearly an hour and a half later the balloon landed at North Petherton.

1829 An Exeter schoolboy swallowed 25 marbles 'out of bravado'.

stand ordinary winters without protection. Take cuttings from Chinas roses. Plant snowdrops, crocuses, Persian iris, narcissus, crown imperials, and dog's

SEPTEMBER

1829 In Tiverton a boy tried to hide in an outhouse after stealing walnuts and died from 'excessive alarm'.

1870 An inch of rain fell at Lynton in twenty minutes.

1882 A thirteen-year old boy of Plymouth was awarded a certificate for saving a life from drowning.

◈ 8 ◈
Nativity of the Virgin Mary

1458 An agreement was reached between the Mayor of Exeter and a canon of the Cathedral for cleaning dirt and filth from a lane near the Close and the city walls.

1564 Richard Payne was warned if he returned to Exeter he would be whipped and have an ear nailed to the pillory.

1831 To celebrate the coronation of William IV there was donkey racing at Sidmouth and at Tiverton flags were flown made from local lace.

1882 Poor children in Plymouth were given a trip to the Eddystone and pasties for lunch.

◈ 9 ◈

1568 The Merchant Adventurers of Exeter purchased 96 lots in the National Lottery with the first prize being £5,000.

1675 Mary Nute was paid four shillings at Sydenham for gathering hops and three weeks' work in the kitchen.

1726 A reward of five pounds was offered for John Whitrow, described as being about 25 years old, wearing a wig and with a fresh scar on his face, accused of murdering an Exeter woman.

tooth violets. Gather any desirable seeds whenever they ripen. ❊ *1898 – Sow a few salads for late crops; lettuce and spinach, if not done last month, for spring*

SEPTEMBER

1848 The *Haberdine* of Teignmouth returned with a cargo of dried cod from Indian Tickle, Labrador.

1848 A swarm of bees settled on confectionary goods in a Honiton market stall.

1852 Death of the Reverend John Froude, hunting parson of Knowstone.

1870 Wealthy French refugees arrived in Exeter fleeing from war on the continent.

❧ 10 ❦

1642 A mob rose at the market cross when Royalists came to South Molton to read the King's Commission of Array.

1725 Mr Clowes of Cheshire performed Royal Sword Dancing at the New Inn at Exeter.

1810 The Eddystone Lighthouse was lit with oil.

1879 The Exmouth Regatta finished with a gig and punt chase, swimming for bladders and a greasy pole contest.

❧ 11 ❦

1641 The Countess of Bath spent six pence in a game of bowls at Tawstock.

1792 It was reported from Bideford that an entire pack of hounds was destroyed owing to madness.

1848 Palmer's Company of Ethiopian Serenaders performed at Exeter.

1871 The ex-Emperor Napoleon began a visit to Torquay and was greeted at the train station with cries of *Vive l'Empereur*.

crops. Plant endive and lettuce. Lift onions and lay them on a dry border or gravel walk. Lift potatoes and store them. Gather and store carefully the autumnal

SEPTEMBER

✦ 12 ✦

Birthday of Agatha Christie, novelist: born at Torquay, 1890.

1848 Engineers surveyed Sidmouth with a view to constructing a harbour.

1869 A schooner was lost in a strong gale on Barnstaple Bar.

1883 It was reported that a letter arrived in Topsham 7 years and 3 months after being sent from Lisbon.

✦ 13 ✦

1505 The Dean and Chapter gave ten shillings to the King's players for a performance.

1630 Lewis Jackson, London merchant, arrived at Southampton with news that two Exeter men had died while exploring the South America.

1806 Nineteen prisoners were housed at the County Prison for Debtors.

1831 (13th–14th) Large numbers of pilchards were seen off Dawlish and Teignmouth.

1869 A heavy gale at Great Torrington covered pear trees with what was suspected to be salt water.

✦ 14 ✦

1584 Sir Francis Drake set sail from Plymouth on a voyage for the West Indies.

1648 Devon laws regarding alehouses, begging and the poor were tightened.

sorts of apples and pears. Continue the propagation of herbaceous plants. Plant evergreens. Keep down weeds. ❋ 1900 – *Keep the hoe busy between the advanc-*

SEPTEMBER

1726 A bright bay horse, 14 hands high with the mark JN on the near buttock, was stolen in Topsham.

1752 Calendar Reform: after a delay of 250 years England adopted the continental New Style calendar and dropped eleven days from the calendar – changing what would have been the 3rd of September to the 14th.

1764 Chagford's rector was accused of immorality and drunkeness.

1766 A six-week old baby, found in a basket on an Exeter doorstop, was sent to the Workhouse.

1974 The South Devon coast path was officially opened.

❧ 15 ❧

1706 (15th–16th) Three men and two women, who had died from drowning, were buried in Barnstaple.

1845 A Tiverton woman returned three bags of potatoes because she believed the world would end in three weeks' time.

1870 Rumours were quashed that the French Empress was recently at St David's Station in Exeter.

1882 Pepper's Ghost Company performed in Exeter.

❧ 16 ❧

1685 Baptism of John Gay, poet, in Barnstaple.

1766 There was civil unrest in Exeter over high grain prices and arrests were made following the theft of a large quantity of cheese from a warehouse at the White Hart.

ing winter crops. Earth up celery. Onions will be ready to draw. Take up potatoes as soon as ripe. Sow the winter crop of spinach. Gather any kinds of apples and

SEPTEMBER

1823 The foundation stone, which weighed nearly two tons, was laid of Honiton's new market house.

1834 Cholera returned to Devon.

1870 Two 'whale-thrashers' were caught off Teignmouth.

⤚ 17 ⤙

St Lambert's Day

Birthday of Samuel Prout, landscape artist: born at Plymouth, 1783.

Election of Plymouth's Mayor (until 1803).

1633 Licenses were granted to Walter Gest to teach grammar at West Alvington, John Francis to teach arithmetic and writing at Dartmouth and Richard Lovett to teach English language and writing at Townstall.

1767 Mr Peckett of York oversaw the placing of his stained glass in the West Window of the Cathedral.

1882 The bathing train from Exeter to Exmouth was crowded and a female visitor from Dawlish attracted attention by swimming ¼ of a mile from the shore.

1882 An old lady fell out of a window, while sleeping, with fatal results in Plymouth.

1915 A flag day in Exeter for the Royal National Lifeboat Institution.

1944 Crowds cheered the ending of black-out in Exeter's High Street.

pears which may ripen this month. Various hardy annuals if sown now will stand ordinary winters without protection. Plant auriculas in their winter

SEPTEMBER

❧ 18 ❦

1821　A recipe for 'the bowel complaint' in *The Alfred – West of England Gazette* called for twelve grains of rhubarb and four grains of ginger in one ounce of peppermint water.

1845　North Devon's harvest of wheat, barley and oats was reportedly adequate whereas potatoes were noted as 'a complete failure'.

1871 (18th–19th)　Heavy rain fell in Ashburton.

❧ 19 ❦

1559　Five Salcombe men were lost at sea.

1592　A London official discovered that the cargo of a rich prize ship at Dartmouth had been plundered.

1936　An open-air baptism was held in the river Taw at Barnstaple.

❧ 20 ❦

1827　Hussey's Black Grease beat Broom's Broom in a trotting match near Cullompton.

1848　Dahlias were exhibited in a public show at the Higher Market in Exeter.

1923　The annual meeting was held of the Devonian Society of Montreal.

1943　*Tarzan Triumphs* played at the Exeter Savoy.

1948　Football was banned from Paignton's public pleasure grounds.

quarters. Edgings of box and thrift or sea daisy may be made new or repaired. ❀ *1901 – Take up potatoes as soon as they are ripe. Plant out coleworts.*

SEPTEMBER

Ember Days (the Wednesday, Friday and Saturday after Holy-Rood Day / the Feast of the Exultation of the Holy Cross, viz. September 14th)

❧ 21 ❧

Wetting the Candle
(held to mark the seasonal change in
the traditional shoe-makers' hours)

1516   Thomas Fuller of Exeter was imprisoned for 40 days for his abusive language.

1597   Freedom Day. Wine, apples and bread were purchased by the town of Plymouth for the annual celebrations.

1826   Abraham Cann of Colebrook defeated James Warren of Redruth in a wrestling contest in London.

1829   It was reported that a thief, interrupted in a Frithelstock garden, left behind two ducks freshly killed but not plucked.

Provide against Michaelmas, bargain to make, for term to give over, to keep or to take; In doing of either, let wit bear a stroke, for buying or selling of pig in a poke.
Thomas Tusser, 1557

❧ 22 ❧

1285   William and Benedictus Dodderigg agreed to block up their doors adjoining the Cathedral churchyard.

1640   Jaspar Tucker was alleged to have called John Baker of Ottery St Mary a whore-master and bastard-maker.

1796   An explosion completely destroyed the *Amphion*, killed some 300 people onboard and the noise caused panic throughout Plymouth.

1845   Eight women and one man were dipped in the river Lowman at Ham Mills Bridge near Tiverton in order to receive salvation before the end of the world (which was predicted in a few weeks time by two men).

1851   A rowing match took place from the Great Tree at Exmouth to the pier of the Starcross railway station.

Plant out lettuces to stand till winter in sheltered situations. Gather any apples or pears which may ripen this month. Various hardy annuals if sown now will

SEPTEMBER

❧ 23 ❧

1648 Hop gatherers at Tawstock received five pence a day for their labour.

1789 The *Providence, Three Brothers, Dolphin, Elizabeth* and *Hudson* were auctioned at Dartmouth.

1877 A new reredos of Bath stone at Clyst Honiton church, executed by Harry Hems, was inaugurated.

1927 1.3 inches of rain fell in Chagford in ten minutes.

1942 Mrs Dorothy Elmhirst of Dartington, 'American Social and Educational Worker', spoke on 'Our American Allies' at Topsham.

❧ 24 ❧

Astrological Sign of LIBRA, the Scales
(through to October 23rd)

1633 Barnstaple shipowners were forced to buy Cornish grain because of potential shortages to local people.

1815 A waterspout passed from Dawlish to Sidmouth.

1824 African teakwood was suspected to have caused the recent deaths of a surgeon, eight shipwrights and two sawyers reported at Plymouth.

1926 Dartington School opened.

❧ 25 ❧

1833 It was reported that the lighthouse on Prawle Point had been erected.

stand ordinary winters without protection. Take cuttings from Chinas roses. Plant snowdrops, crocuses, Persian iris, narcissus, crown imperials, and dog's

SEPTEMBER

1839 The *Peamore*, a schooner of 260 tons, was launched at Topsham.

1871 Three inches of rain fell in Kingsbridge.

1882 Mr W. Irving Bishop, 'the distinguished thought-reader and anti-spiritualist', performed in Exeter.

❧ 26 ❧

1580 The *Golden Hind* sailed into Plymouth after a three-year voyage which encompassed the globe and Drake's first question was reportedly 'Is the Queen still alive'?

1806 The Exeter County High Gaol for Felons housed 31 prisoners whereas in Tiverton Bridewell there were two women, one of whom had been there for three years waiting to be transported overseas.

1877 Lady Georgina Fortescue of Castle Hill married Lord Ernest James Seymour at Filleigh and among the presents were an Indian Shawl, Worcester tea service, pony carriage, half a dozen gold scissors, seal-skin purse, and Macaulay's *Essays*.

1882 Dr Seaton, 'the Wizard of the World', performed his Hindu Mysteries, Chinese Feats and Mesmerism in Tiverton.

❧ 27 ❧

1609 The *Seraphin* of Exmouth arrived at Topsham from New-foundland with fish and train oil.

1840 Fire at the Royal Dockyard caused damage to ships and buildings estimated at £200,000.

1849 It was reported that shops in Exeter would shortly close at

tooth violets. Gather any desirable seeds whenever they ripen. ❋ *1907 – Sow vegetable seeds for a spring crop, and plant German greens, savoys, celery,*

SEPTEMBER

7pm because of an increased realisation that 'human beings have other faculties to cultivate, other purposes to accomplish' than only work.

1872 The water quality of the South Teign at Yeo Bridge was judged as being 'slightly turbid'.

1877 It was reported that a humorous lecture resulted in an hour of continuous laughter at the Exeter Literary Society.

❧ 28 ❧

1581 Henry Mugg, pirate, was hanged in chains on Start Point.

1824 Gas pipes were being laid at Devonport.

1829 A melon weighing nearly 21 pounds was reportedly cut in the Dock Yard.

1877 It was announced that a benefit would be held in Teignmouth for Master Corelli Windeatt, a six and one half year old violinist, to aid his musical education.

❧ 29 ❧

Quarter Day Michaelmas
(St Michael the Archangel)

Swearing in of the mayor of Plymouth (until 1803)

1524 At Tiverton Castle the cook for Katherine, Countess of Devon, used in the kitchen two geese, roast beef, a pig, two capons, eight chickens, butter, eggs, milk, cream and apples for tarts.

1763 Henry White of Widecombe, described as being 24 years

lettuces, and perennial, aromatic and pot herbs. Hoe winter spinach and turnips, earth up celery and cardoons, prick out cabbage plants, gather ripe seeds, and

SEPTEMBER

old, five foot seven inches high, short brown hair, grey eyes and with a fresh complexion, was wanted for deserting His Majesty's Royal Regiment of Fusiliers.

1831 At the exhibition of the Devon Horticultural Society the prize for best-flavoured pineapple was awarded to Mr Craggs, gardener at Killerton, with second prize going to Mr Glendenning, gardener at Bicton.

1882 The editor of *The Western Times* reported that Edith O'Gormon, 'The Escaped Nun', who had given three lectures (one to women only) had created considerable excitement in Exeter but bad feeling among Roman Catholics.

1900 In Ilfracombe, 2½ inches of rain fell in 45 minutes.

1918 Fourteen American soldiers, who died at Oldway Hospital of pneumonia, were buried with military honours at Paignton.

❧ 30 ❧

1829 The foundation stone for 'Loop Hoon Cottage' in South Molton was laid.

1839 The apple crop in the neighbourhood of Barnstaple was reported as being 'far more productive than was expected'.

1864 A mushroom, weighing one pound and measuring ten inches across, was found in Tiverton.

1938 *The Western Times* reported that a peace agreement was signed in Berlin.

1948 Ex-GI jackets were on sale in Exeter for fifteen shillings.

---

make mushroom beds. Plant cuttings of currants, raspberries, gooseberries, and strawberries. Make cuttings of scarlet geraniums, calceolarias, verbenas. ✿✿✿

OCTOBER

October good blast,
To blow the hog mast.

Thomas Tusser, 1557

OCTOBER

❧ 1 ❧

1605 A licence was granted to Arthur Southcot of Shillingford, gentleman, for shooting a 'handgun and birding piece at any crow, chough, pierook, ringtail, jay or smaller birds for hawk's meat only'.

1636 Orders were issued for better behaviour in the Cathedral and churchyard. The scandals included 'crying and unquietness and the unreasonable playing and running about of children' during services in addition to the playing of sports within the churchyard.

1685 It was decided that the heads and quarters of the traitors who rebelled with the Duke of Monmouth were to be sent to Axminster, Barnstaple, Bideford, Colyton, Crediton, Dartmouth, Honiton, Plymouth, Tiverton, Torrington and Totnes.

1725 Six guineas was the asking price at Sampford Courtenay for Captain Dunning's machines which prevented the overturning of coaches.

1948 HMS *Loch Eck* was handed over at Devonport to New Zealand and renamed HMNZS *Hawea*.

1951 Douglas Fairbanks Junior featured in *Mr Drake's Duck* at The Cinema, Torrington.

❧ 2 ❧

1501 Katherine, daughter of Ferdinand, King of Spain, landed at Plymouth en route to marry Arthur, Prince of Wales, in London.

1503 Agnes Oryng's servant was pronounced a 'common strumpet' at Dartmouth.

✸✸✸ 1891 – *Plant lettuces, horseradishes, early cabbages, and other greens neglected last month, in sheltered places; also cauliflowers, mint, and tarragon,*

OCTOBER

1655   Eight shoemakers agreed that they would not work for less than four shillings per week in Exeter or elsewhere.

1766   Knightshayes, a farm near Tiverton which would make a 'very agreeable spot for a gentleman's seat', was auctioned at The Tuns in Tiverton.

1821   A new coach called 'The Traveller' was advertised to leave Cathedral Yard in Exeter every evening at 4.45 and arrive in Birmingham at seven o'clock the next night.

❧ 3 ❧

1792   It was reported from Exeter that 'the celebrated' Dr Graham had given a series of lectures 'on his newly adapted systems of earth-bathing, in a garden on Southernhay where he exhibited to his numerous auditors himself buried up to chin for several hours'.

1830   It was reported from Starcross that a 'rare and curious fish called the European Angler, Toad Fish or Sea Devil, was caught in three feet of water, the fish measured 4½ feet long and three feet in breadth'.

1846   It was reported that the *Haberdine* of Teignmouth arrived home from Indian Tickle, Labrador with the first fish of the season.

1848   The Plympton House Lunatic Asylum was advertised as 'a desirable residence for invalids of the higher and middle classes of society'.

1938   The first public spelling bee was held in Crediton.

1944   The town of Sidmouth searched for a Town Crier (who would have an annual salary of £5).

in frames, for winter use. Earth up savoys and cabbages as high as the leaves. Take up carrots and parsnips, cut off their tops, and bury them in dry sand. Crop

OCTOBER

❧ 4 ❧

Birthday of William Bligh, later 'Breadfruit Bligh', Captain of the *Bounty*: born at Plymouth, 1754

1809 At the General Court of Governors of the Exeter Lunatic Asylum it was reported that 40 patients remained of whom 23 were better and 17 'not worse than when admitted'.

1812 First meeting of the Plymouth Institution (later called the Plymouth Athenaeum).

1820 It was announced that the Devon and Exeter Female Penitentiary was to reopen as a Refuge for the Deserted and Helpless Victims of Man's Seduction.

1880 (4th–5th) At Babbacombe continuous rain fell from 5 a.m. to midnight with showers until 8.50 a.m. on the 5th, 2.44 inches of rain fell.

1918 An Ashburton dairyman was fined for milk containing eighteen per cent water.

❧ 5 ❧

1623 Prince Charles and the Duke of Buckingham returned from Spain without securing a marriage agreement with the Spanish Infanta and at Exeter it was noted that bonfires were lit in celebration.

1829 A 'Glory of the West', measuring fifteen inches in circumference, was grown in Pilton.

1830 A lecture on slavery was given at the Exeter Assembly Rooms.

1833 A Plymouth woman died from scratches received while trying to drown her pet cat.

1918 Okehampton was without gas owing to a shortage of coal.

the tops of parsley, to make fresh leaves for winter. Begin pruning, taking the vertical branches in fruit trees and cutting obliquely to keep rain from lodging.

OCTOBER

❧ 6 ❧

1497 Henry VII arrived in Tiverton on his journey to Exeter.

1620 Michael Heyman of Whimple, labourer, admitted playing cards for cider at the house of John Blake in Larkbeare and later at quoits in Larkbeare Green but denied any wrongdoing.

1763 Richard Gorden sold cabinet and chairs 'after the latest fashion' at the Mahogany Tree in Exeter.

1863 An earthquake was felt throughout Devon at around three in the morning.

1882 It was reported that Mr Harwood of Tiverton won first prize for his Minorca cock at the Dairy Show in London.

❧ 7 ❧

1497 Henry VII arrived in Exeter.

1611 It began to rain at Exeter and continued for five days 'so that Exe was very big and did overflow the country up and down, the Thursday at night between 10 a clock till 4 a clock the next morning it was at highest. It did much hurt at Exe Bridge and in their houses and barns & up most part St Thomas parish the like flood never seen by the memory of man'.

1938 The first honeymoon couple to leave Exeter airport flew to Weston Super Mare.

❧ 8 ❧

1607 A county collection was made to ransom a Plymouth-born captive of the Turks who was serving in a galley; a collector

Plant all deciduous trees and shrubs. ✽ *1896 – Continue to take up potatoes when the weather is suitable. Earth up celery in fine dry weather, and ridge or*

OCTOBER

was to stand at the doorway of every church after divine service to solicit contributions.

1625 Charles I viewed the naval expedition at Plymouth for Cadiz, the first visit by a reigning monarch to Devon for more than a hundred years.

1672 The *Torrington Merchant* arrived safely at Ilfracombe from Newfoundland with passengers and fish oil.

1725 Ann Dejoux, widow of the French minister at Plymouth, offered lessons in painting on glass, waxwork, shell work and in the making of paper flowers.

1767 Exeter gossiped over 'The Tiverton Beauty' giving a lock of hair to an officer who made a ring in which it was enclosed with the engraving 'My hair is in thee, My heart is with thee'.

❧ 9 ❦

1792 The *Sophia*, a copper-bottomed vessel built by John Stephens, was launched at Ringmore.

1815 A group of 22 persons met in a Shebbear farmhouse, precursors to the Bible Christians.

1835 Mr Veitch exhibited a collection of dahlias at the Devon & Exeter Floricultural Society exhibition. Among those particularly noted were Veitch's Mars (cupped scarlet) and the National (white with purple stripes through each petal).

1852 It was lamented in *The Western Times* that a train from Exeter to Plymouth was one hour late: 'such casualties as are bearable if not of frequent occurrence, but when the rule is for the train to be nearly an hour late, at least four days out of seven, it is of course regarded as the exception when it comes to time'.

dig any ground as soon as it is vacant. Parsnips and carrots should be taken up when their tops turn yellow. Store apples and pears. Begin the pruning of

OCTOBER

❧ 10 ❧

1611 Burial of Adam Wyatt, the Barnstaple Chronicler.

1792 It was announced that The Western Bank would be established in Exeter in January 1793.

1806 There were 9 inmates at the Plymouth Town Gaol.

1832 Plymouth and Stonehouse observed a day of Thanksgiving for the end of the cholera epidemic.

1845 The world failed to end as predicted by two visionaries in Tiverton.

❧ 11 ❧

1823 John Cooke, landlord of the Lord Nelson public-house in Exeter, was prosecuted for selling cider without a licence.

1832 The Plymouth Naval Club held a dinner to celebrate the victory of Camperdown.

1877 Large numbers of mackerel were caught at Dawlish and Teignmouth.

❧ 12 ❧

1591 The news reached Barnstaple of the death of Sir Richard Grenville and the long battle of the *Revenge*. The town clerk noted the ship 'encountered with the whole Spanish fleet being 70 sail whereof they slew many men but were fain to yield at last upon composition for their lives and liberties'.

1766 Two American preachers, one of whom was an ordained Mohican, solicited financial support in Exeter for teaching native American children.

gooseberries and currant bushes; transplant them about the end of the month. Strawberry beds should be top dressed with well-rotted manure. ❋ 1898 – Sow

OCTOBER

1829 It was reported that a large portion of the cliff at East Teignmouth fell into the sea.

1880 Complaints were made that swans were swimming without permission in the Pounds Reservoirs in Plymouth.

❧ 13 ❦

1832 It was reported in *The Devonshire Chronicle and Exeter News* that a Cornish family died after mistaking oak fungus for mushrooms.

1837 Incorporation of Devonport as a borough.

1845 The brother of Miss Appletree of Sidmouth managed to stop her elopement at Exeter railway station.

❧ 14 ❦

1726 Sir William Pole of Shute offered a reward for the return of his five-month old fallow-coloured fox hound with a white garland around its neck and four white feet.

1759 William Criddle, Cullompton cloth-maker, insured his property for £100.

1823 Hackney coaches were brought to Exeter 'as an experiment'.

1845 Miss Appletree of Sidmouth claimed her recent elopement was intended as a hoax.

1877 A storm caused massive destruction throughout southern England and in Pinhoe a falling chimney stack killed one woman.

1914 The Canadian volunteer army arrived unannounced at Plymouth in more than 30 ships.

small salads and radishes in the first week; Mazagan beans and early frame peas in the last week. Plant cabbages in beds or close rows till wanted in spring.

OCTOBER

❧ 15 ❧

1631 A Navy captain wrote to the Privy Council that a French ship, after having been supplied with victuals at Plymouth, came ashore and stole 12 sheep, an ox and 'robbed, pillaged and stripped' the local fishermen.

1727 Three Ottery St Mary nurseries, with Dutch elm, horse chestnut and cherry trees, were for sale.

1823 The Assembly Ball at Plymouth drew a large fashionable crowd of 'bewitching belles, all-attentive beaux and matronly spectators'.

1831 A large flock of swallows flew south from Plymouth Sound.

❧ 16 ❧

1759 Light was first shown on the new Eddystone Lighthouse.

1827 The Subscription, a post coach, advertised its schedule from Exeter to Bristol but assured readers of *The Alfred* that 'no fish carried to the annoyance of passengers'.

1845 It was reported that two time periods were displayed on the new dial at St John's Church in Exeter: a silver minute hand showed 'railway time' and a gilt hand showed the 'true time' with several minutes between them.

❧ 17 ❧

Birthday of Sir John Bowring, writer and traveller: born at Exeter, 1792

1562 Expenses for Braunton's church ale included baking bread and pies, making clothes for Robin Hood and his men and the brewing ale.

Store potatoes, beet, carrots, parsnips, etc., by the end of the month. This is the best season for transplanting fruit trees. Plant the greater part of the common

OCTOBER

1580 Mary Feres and Joan Allen died of the plague in Barnstaple.

1780 Death of William Cookworthy, porcelain maker, China clay discoverer and founder of Plymouth China.

1789 The household servants at Saltram were unhappy about the use of the house in the summer by the Royal Family.

1864 It was reported that a machine dug up 400 bags of potatoes in less than seven hours in Monkokehampton.

❧ 18 ❧

1656 The food in the kitchen at Sydenham included 3 tarts, a turkey pie, lumber pie, giblet pie and quince pie.

1820 The public was cautioned that swindlers were in the county with pound notes altered to ten pounds.

1831 Thomas Hake, proprietor of the Russia Fur Manufactory in Exeter, offered to keep ladies' muffs and tippets safe from moths during the summer months.

1928 Grant of a title of a city by George V to Plymouth.

❧ 19 ❧

1670 Enquiries were made at Thorverton by Joseph Tribridge, yeoman, concerning a hen of his, described as 'a white guinea with reddish feathers upon the wings', which he suspected had been eaten by a neighbour.

1814 The claim by Joanna Southcott of Exeter, prophet to some, that she was about to give birth to the Prince of Peace prompted crowds to gather in London to welcome the baby.

1875 The Lowman flooded in Tiverton causing the death of a

border bulbs about the end of the month. ❀ *1900 – Transplant August sown lettuce. Take up parsnips and carrots. Continue to take up potatoes. Hand-*

OCTOBER

labourer by the name of Sweet; the flood waters carried him from the back of his horse and he drowned in the waters.

1880 Snow fell on Haldon Hill.

❧ 20 ❧

1629 Katherine Small allegedly slandered Alice Churchill of Malborough by saying 'she is a whore and she hath played the whore with a man of war'.

1753 Cadeleigh's rector was accused of saying there was 'no harm' in fornication between two people in the same social class.

1803 No prisoners were held in the Town Gaol at Tiverton whereas in the Bridewell there were four Frenchmen and one woman waiting to be transported overseas.

1831 A gannet was shot at Hooe Lake near Plymouth.

1877 A pet cat woke its owners at night to save them from a fire raging in their house in Honiton.

❧ 21 ❧

Birthday of S.T. Coleridge, poet and philosopher: born at Ottery St Mary, 1772.

1501 Catherine of Aragon arrived in Exeter en route to marry the Prince of Wales.

1618 The *Laurel* of Dartmouth returned from a voyage to the Amazon with a rich cargo.

1638 A great storm hit Widecombe; 'in the time of Divine Service a strange darkness, increasing more and more, so that the people there assembled could not see to read in any book,

weed spinach; earth-up celery. Commence pruning gooseberries and currant bushes; they may also be transplanted towards the end of the month. Place all

and suddenly in a fearful and lamentable manner, a mighty thundering was heard' followed by lightning and a 'great ball of fire come in at the window and pass through the Church with a great cry of burning and scalding, they all giving themselves up for dead'.

1846 Honora Scarroll, a woman of 'doubtful reputation', drowned after visiting the *Stromboli* in the Hamoaze late at night. Several crewmembers later admitted to having heard a splash as she left.

1880 Five inches of snow fell in Exeter.

✦ 22 ✦

Birthday of James Northcote, painter: born at Plymouth, 1746.

1629 Richard Taylor allegedly accused Hugh Wyott of 'keeping three men's wives in Braunton'.

1725 A booksale was held at Dick's Coffee House in Exeter.

1827 A mushroom was gathered in Paignton measuring nine inches and three quarters across.

1918 It was reported that £250 had been raised in Paignton for the French Red Cross.

1975 Opening of the Westcountry Studies Library at Exeter.

✦ 23 ✦

1788 The Scots Pine plantation at Saltram was being felled.

1845 It was announced that Mrs Dexter, the 'far famed champion

plants requiring protection in the turf-pit. Bulbs intended for flowering in the window during the early spring should now be potted. Prune roses. ✽ 1901 –

OCTOBER

of the ladies dress reform', would be lecturing in Exeter in 'full and genuine Bloomer costume'.

1868 The Queen of Holland arrived for a fortnight's visit to Torquay.

1918 Exeter's City Treasurer reported that only one person on the city's payroll was of 'enemy origin'.

❧ 24 ❧

Astrological Sign of SCORPIO, the Scorpion
(through to November 22nd)

1820 Two swindlers, one called Smith (tall, brown hair, light eyes and with a scar on his head) and the other Harris (shorter, dark hair and eyes, with 'somewhat of a Jewish physiognomy') were operating in the Exeter area with a false story of ship-wreck.

1823 The sale of Lord Courtenay's furniture at Powderham continued with much of the contents of the Music Room reportedly purchased by Lord Rolle.

1870 (24th–25th) The aurora borealis seen at Zeal Monachorum.

❧ 25 ❧
St Crispin's Day

1558 Margaret Fox of Dartmouth answered charges of witchcraft by testifying she did not believe witches had supernatural powers and claimed she moved from Malborough to Modbury, Woodleigh, Cornwood and finally Dartmouth because of malicious gossip which followed her from one place to another.

Continue to take up potatoes when the weather is suitable. Earth up celery in fine dry weather, and ridge or dig any ground as soon as it is vacant. Parsnips

OCTOBER

1823 On display at the Swan Theatre, Exeter, was the Wild Indian Venus whose 'complexion is of a copper colour, hair a jet black, straight and stiff. Her head is of a peculiar form: the tips of her ears rest on her shoulders. To her ears and her lower lip she had a circular piece of wood most curiously attached. Though under the middle stature, she is extremely well proportioned, is about 30 years of age and was considered a complete Venus in her native country. She is decently attired and perfectly kind to strangers'.

1848 The Mayor of Exeter gave notice that tar barrels and masks would no longer be allowed in the celebrations on November 5.

1859 (25th–26th) A great storm hit the West Country causing widespread damage.

1918 Schools in the Newton Abbot area were closed because of an outbreak of influenza.

❧ 26 ❧

1809 Doctor Dunn, of London, who received patients in Exeter for blindness, deafness, ruptures and cancers, made it a rule to 'reject the incurable and to inform every patient, or their friends, at first sight, whether a perfect cure, or what degree of relief can be expected'.

1817 A woodcock was caught in a gallery in Bideford church.

1835 The Crediton Ploughing Match took place in Jews Hollacombe Barton with 17 ploughs, 12 driven by men and 5 by boys.

1944 The Red Cross and St John Book Campaign held its Great Devonshire Book Drive at Ilfracombe.

and carrots should be taken up when their tops turn yellow. Store apples and pears. Begin the pruning of gooseberries and currant bushes; transplant them

OCTOBER

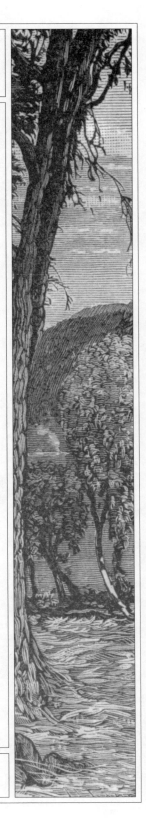

❧ 27 ❦

1820 A new bypass for Okehampton was celebrated with a public procession.

1857 *Woolmer's Exeter and Plymouth Gazette* reported a 'respectable attendance' at the annual meeting of the Exeter Auxiliary Bible Society.

1877 The Dean & Chapter gave a dinner for workmen restoring the Cathedral.

1913 A hailstorm in the Culm Valley from Silverton to Uffculme caused widespread damage.

❧ 28 ❦

1576 At Halberton two shillings and six pence were paid for 'a fud ball – football – and a dozen of bowls'.

1829 A gooseberry bush was in full flower in South Molton.

1918 New ration regulations allowed one ounce of butter and four of margarine per person weekly.

❧ 29 ❦

1618 Sir Walter Raleigh, explorer, adventurer, courtier and poet among his many talents, was executed at Westminster. Among the witnesses was Sir John Eliot who later wrote 'Such was his unmoved courage and placid temper that, while it changed the affection of the enemies who had come to witness it, and turned their joy to sorrow, it filled all men else with emotion and admiration, leaving them only with this doubt – whether death were more acceptable to him or he more welcome unto death'.

about the end of the month. Strawberry beds should be top dressed with well-rotted manure. ❁ *1907 – Plant lettuces, horseradish, early cabbages and other*

OCTOBER

1725 A reward of one guinea was offered for the return of a black rusty mare, 4 to 5 years old, 15 hands high, marked with an X by the near pin, with a large white streak over the face, snip over the nose, three white feet, a full mane of hair and a swink tail.

1795 Flood waters in Barnstaple reached as far as the Golden Lion Inn.

1877 A flock of ten Canada Geese was seen near Plymouth.

1918 Raleigh Tercentenary. Meetings were held in Exeter, London, Woolwich, Jersey and Raleigh.

❧ 30 ❦

1570 At the time of his death Richard Tailor alias Farringdon of Exeter, cordwainer, had in his shop 100 pairs of women's shoes valued at seven pence a pair, 116 pairs of men's shoes worth twelve pence a pair and 71 pairs of childrens' shoes valued at five pence a pair.

1863 It was reported that Messrs. Lucombe Pince & Co. of Exeter was given a first class certificate by the London Horticultural Society for 'Mrs Pince's Black Muscat'.

1868 An earthquake was felt in the county.

1875 The steamship *Newcomin* ran aground on mud just below Totnes.

1918 Three of the ten cases before the Devon Assizes involved bigamy.

1944 The Great Devonshire Book Drive moved to Seaton.

greens, neglected last month, in sheltered places; also cauliflowers, mint and tarragon in frames, for winter use. Earth up savoys and cabbages as high as the

OCTOBER

✍ 31 ✍

1817 A thunderstorm struck Holsworthy.

1831 A Fancy Ball was held at Teignmouth and it was reported 'the whole affair went off with great eclat'. Among those attending were Captain Dashwood in an Albanian costume, Mr Fry as 'a Jew', Dr West as Figaro, Mr Stephenson as a Spanish Don and 'amongst the ladies were Nuns who had taken the veil, Sultanas, Flower Girls and there was a very excellent group of three sisters and a friend as Norman Peasants, Sylphs, Swiss Peasants and Zephyrs'.

1852 A large number of trawling boys gathered outside Brixham church, interrupted the service, mocked the minister and tore his gown.

leaves. Take up carrots and parsnips, cut off their tops and bury them in dry sand. Crop the tops of parsley to make new fresh leaves for the winter. ❋❋❋

169]

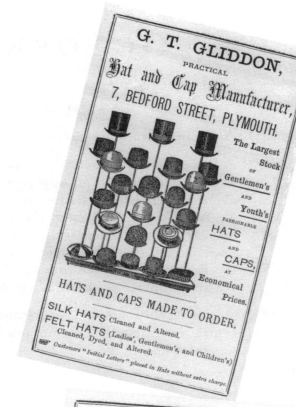

NOVEMBER

November take flail;
Let ship no more sail.

Thomas Tusser, 1557

NOVEMBER

❧ 1 ❧
All Hallows Day / All Saints' Day

1514 The church bells were rung at Ashburton.

1835 A large flock of swallows were seen flying south from Plymouth.

1845 Navvies working on the South Devon Railway disagreed with the contractor over wages and laid siege to his office.

1877 It was reported 16,868 washers and 7,398 bathers used the Exeter Bath and Washhouses in the last year.

1949 Large crowds greeted the return to Plymouth of HMS *Amethyst* from service in China on the Yangtse River.

❧ 2 ❧
All Souls' Day

1600 Death of Richard Hooker, Exeter theologian and author of *The Laws of Ecclesiastical Politie*, following a journey along the river Thames.

1642 A woman was overheard saying she would burn her house down before allowing the Exeter's constables to search it.

1800 Humphry Repton, landscape designer, was in a dispute at Saltram over his fee.

1857 Opening of the Torquay Working Men's Improvement Society.

❧ 3 ❧

1285 Two carpenters repaired a choir door in Exeter Cathedral.

❀❀❀ 1896 – *Double blossoming frame peas may now be sown under a fence or wall. Sow early Lisbon beans in a sheltered situation, and a light soil. This is*

NOVEMBER

1572   Richard Packhouse of Creacombe admitted he and James Dodge got along 'like two butcher's dogs' and that he wished to be buried in separate churchyards because otherwise they would 'not lie quietly together but rise and scratch and claw together like caterwauling cats'.

1768   There were rumours that Exeter's theatre would soon have a season of Shakespeare plays including *Cymbeline*, *Coriolanus* and *Measure for Measure*.

1865   It was reported in *The Western Times* that 'Young Exeter is preparing for its annual orgies on the Fifth. Arrangements are being made to have the bonfire in Cathedral Yard as usual'.

1865   Dowager Queen Emma, of the Sandwich Islands, visited Torquay on her national tour to raise money to build a cathedral.

1918   Jam was rationed but not syrup or honey.

1934   Field Marshall HRH the Duke of Connaught opened the Connaught Gardens in Sidmouth.

☙ 4 ❧

Custom of 'Halloaing' for biscuits (East Budleigh)

1562   Queen Elizabeth commanded the city of Exeter to provide 500 men for armed service.

1608   A poor grain harvest forced Exeter's mayor to purchase 4,000 bushels of rye for the poor.

1831   The Devon Glee Club held their second meeting of the season at the New London Inn, Exeter.

1847   The Silver Cup for the best 5 acres of Swedish Turnips, given

the best month for pruning or transplanting. Prune and nail fruit trees on walls. Plant hyacinths the first week if possible. Plant tulips in the first week.

NOVEMBER

by J.B. Swete of Oxton House, at the Annual Ploughing Match of the Exminster Farmers Club was awarded to J.B. Swete.

❧ 5 ❧

1611   The Peter Bell at Exeter Cathedral was 'crazed' from ringing.

1643   The Royalists began firing against the defenders of Mount Stamford, one of the main outworks near Parliamentarian Plymouth.

1664   Axminster's bells were rung to mark the Gunpowder Plot (as they were on nearly every year for which there are records).

1688   Brixham's bells rang as William of Orange landed, conveniently coinciding with Bonfire Night.

1831   A Black Stork was shot on the river Tamar.

1845   At Exeter guns were fired, crackers let off, rockets exhibited, bells rung, effigies of Popes carried and a bonfire and tar barrels lit in front of the Cathedral.

1867   Torquay had a bread riot.

1877   A display of electric light took place at the Museum in Exeter, eclipsing the gas lights in the room.

1883   The effigies burnt at Exeter included not just the Pope of Rome but also of General Booth, 'the modern Pope of the Salvation Army'.

❧ 6 ❧

1643   The Royalist onslaught of Mount Stamford continued with soldiers wearing a sprig of bay in their hats or helmets as a

This is the best month for making alterations in the flower garden, which has now quite lost its beauty. ❋ 1898 – *Sow early frame peas and mazagan beans*

NOVEMBER

'sign to be known'. By the end of the afternoon the Parliamentarians had lost, were allowed to 'march out with their muskets and swords and 1 piece of ordnance' and the Cavaliers entered the fort by five o'clock.

1725 Mr Honeywell of Holsworthy sold Squire's Grand Elixir for the treatment of gout and colic.

1830 Thieves entered the larder of James Ley of Bideford and stole a fat goose, a fillet of veal and a large piece of beef.

1869 A meteor was seen at 6 p.m. at Great Torrington.

1882 In Exeter the Gunpowder Plot celebrations occurred a day later (due to the 5th being a Sunday) and the consequence of the bonfire (10 tons of railway sleepers, 20-30 tar barrels and 120 seams of wood) was one man had his fingers burned, three boys and men were injured by 'gunpowder in the face' and one boy had a 'contusion in the forehead through having a burning log thrown at him'.

1936 Mr J. Sneller won an Okehampton competition for guessing a sheep's weight (47 lbs 4 oz.).

✺ 7 ✺

1588 The *San Pedro* came ashore at Hope Cove near Salcombe and became the only Armada ship to be wrecked on the Devon coast.

1633 A prisoner in Plymouth was overheard saying that Queen Elizabeth was 'an old whore'.

1846 It was reported at Plymouth that in the parish of St Andrew there were 180 deaths in the summer quarter, 26 died from consumption, 15 from measles, 15 from diarrhea and 3 from cholera.

in the second week for an early crop. Protect endive, celery, artichokes, and seakale with stable litter or ferns. Mulch asparagus with hot-bed manure. Plant

NOVEMBER

❧ 8 ❧

1560 Braunton's churchwardens gave 2 shillings for 'meat and drink for Robin Hood and his company'.

1792 French refugees were arriving in Exeter.

1814 Snow fell on Dartmoor.

1830 A public meeting was held at Exeter's Guildhall regarding 'Negro Slavery'.

❧ 9 ❧

1605 Nine pence was paid for mending Totnes' hour glass.

1646 Twenty-two men and women received alms at Tawstock.

1650 A Barnstaple apothecary was paid four pounds and twelve shillings.

1912 Victoria Park was officially opened in Bideford.

❧ 10 ❧

1564 In Exeter two women were 'carted' (brought through the streets in a cart to imply loose morals) and banished.

1604 William Honeywell of Rydon purchased a rabbit for eight pence from a vendor named Lightfoot.

1763 An 'Entertainment' was held at Powderham to mark Lord Viscount Courtenay's birthday and coming of age.

1865 Grant Brothers of Torquay advertised Miniature Billiards for sale.

1916 A white and liver-spotted spaniel was lost at Cadbury.

all sorts of fruit-trees in fine weather. Plant dried tubers of border flowers, but the finer sorts had better be delayed till spring. This is the month for repairing

[176

NOVEMBER

❧ 11 ❧

1622 Elizabeth Bradsell of St Sidwell allegedly slandered Elizabeth Berrye by saying 'thou art a punch, a common punch, a base punch and an over-ridden punch and a whore, and thy child is a bastard begotten by a gentleman in a green satin suit'.

1857 Jonathan Roose of Torquay, aged about nineteen years old, was sentenced to penal servitude for murdering Jane Stone who had been pregnant with his child.

1864 An editorial in *The Devon Weekly Times* called for the abolition of Guy Fawkes Night because it revived anti-Catholic sentiments.

1899 Four plum trees and three pear trees were planted in the vicarage garden at Witheridge.

1918 A thanksgiving service was held in Exeter Cathedral to mark the end of the war. Over the Guildhall the Union Jack hung alongside flags of the Allies.

❧ 12 ❧

1595 Sir John Hawkins died at three o'clock in the afternoon in the *Garland* off Puerto Rico.

1622 Agnes Knowling of Dean Prior allegedly called her neighbour 'as common as a dog or a bitch'.

1765 Fire destroyed several houses in Axminster.

1918 Mr and Mrs Benjamin Nodder of Plymouth celebrated their Pearl Wedding Anniversary.

1918 Schools in Dartmouth remained closed due to the influenza outbreak.

1943 Residents of East Allington and Stokenham were informed

drains and renewing fences. ❉ 1900 – *Keep all young crops clean and free from slugs. This is the best month in the year for transplanting. Neither prune*

NOVEMBER

that they had to evacuate their homes for the preparations for D-Day.

❧ 13 ❦

1652 Grace Mathew complained at Exeter that her husband was bewitched. She testified that she was given various remedies by a Broadclyst woman who was 'tall of stature, of a pale face, and blinking eye' and had a staff. The alleged witch was said to have caused further illness and was seen with a toad in her lap and two others at her feet.

1775 An outbreak of influenza travelled east to Okehampton and Ashburton.

1824 It was reported that Exeter's recent celebrations had resulted in several scuffles between the constables and the 'tar barrel worthies'.

1943 Residents of Blackawton and Slapton were informed that they had to evacuate their homes for the preparations for D-Day.

❧ 14 ❦

1640 Twenty-two dozen tiles were purchased at a tuppence each to use in a Tawstock dairy.

1643 The Reverend John Syms left Sheepstor and noted in his journal 'I was forced to leave Shittestor the 14 of November 1643, having been tossed to and fro and forced many times to hide myself the whole year almost before'.

1877 A billiards match was played at the Black Horse Hotel in Exeter.

nor transplant during frosty weather: dull mild weather is best. Prepare all vacant ground, unless it be very light, for future crops. Keep the plants in the pit

NOVEMBER

1931 A Yorkshire Canary won Best Bird in show at the annual exhibition of the Barnstaple and North Devon Cage Bird Society.

❧ 15 ❧

1527 Death at three o'clock in the afternoon of Katherine, the youngest daughter of King Edward IV and the widow of William Courtenay, Earl of Devon, at Tiverton Castle. Her body was embalmed and lay in state for a fortnight until the funeral.

1577 Francis Drake sailed out of Plymouth Sound in late afternoon on his flagship the *Pelican* allegedly destined for Alexandria (and nearly three years later returned from his circumnavigation of the globe).

1792 A Buckfastleigh cloth maker and his wife died suddenly after eating a 'hearty meal'.

1830 The Reverend Luxmoore complained in Barnstaple Guildhall that butchers were openly profaning the Sabbath.

❧ 16 ❧

1725 Mr Brice of Exeter sold a 'fine pleasant prepared tobacco for the head, stomach and sore weak or dim eyes'.

1824 The contents of the missing box of the Sailors' Club at Clovelly were found.

1830 It was reported from Plymouth that the Camera Obscura was 'blown to pieces' by a gale in the morning.

1922 Gunnery practice by HMS *Barham* and HMS *Resolution* was

of window constantly free from dead leaves or mouldiness. Plant hyacinths in the first week if possible. Procure and plant any choice flowering shrubs.

NOVEMBER

blamed for 'atmospheric disturbances' reported throughout Devon.

❧ 17 ❧
Queen Elizabeth's Day

1573 (and through to the end of the century) The bells of Crediton were rung in honour of the birthday of Elizabeth I.

1597 Philip Pallmour and Alice Humfrye were the twentieth couple to marry in Barnstaple that year.

1865 The sighting of three swallows in Withycombe Raleigh was the subject of village talk.

❧ 18 ❧

1539 Exeter's yarn market house was built by selling the cloisters' roof of St Nicholas Priory.

1618 Thomas Docton was buried in Hartland and on his memorial brass was inscribed:

> *Here I lie outside the chancel door,*
> *Here I lie because I am poor;*
> *The further in, the more they pay,*
> *But here lie I as warm as they.*

1775 (18th–19th) The influenza epidemic peaked in Exeter.

1814 Rows of orange and lemon trees in full fruit decorated a birthday fete at Farringdon House.

❧ 19 ❧

1633 Exeter officials allocated ten pounds for a clock with chimes on the Great Conduit.

✾ 1901 – *Double blossoming frame peas may now be sown under a fence or wall. Sow early Lisbon beans in a sheltered situation, and a light soil. This is*

NOVEMBER

1817 Exeter's shops were shut to mourn Princess Charlotte.

1918 *My Four years in Germany* was shown in Victoria Hall, Exeter.

1929 At Holne 4.59 inches of rain fell in 24 hours.

❧ 20 ❧

1330 An Exeter canon agreed to repair his property in Winkleigh.

1651 Jacob Jackson of Rotterdam was fined for firing guns from his ship at Plymouth.

1673 Elizabeth Flay was buried in her husband's grave nearly forty years after he died.

1703 The Great Storm of 1703: one casualty was Henry Winstanley who was responsible for building the lighthouse situated, until that storm, on the Eddystone.

1863 It was reported that nearly every hedge in Exmouth was covered with primroses in full bloom.

1934 Swallows were seen at Prawle Point.

❧ 21 ❧

1566 Four men in Exeter were whipped for playing cards and other games.

1639 Complaints were made about Hartland's cleric who refused to baptise a newly-born baby who was ill and died the following day. He was said to have responded 'shit Gossip the child is dead'.

1815 The Exeter Gas Light Company began laying pipes.

the best month for pruning or transplanting. Prune and nail fruit trees on walls. Plant hyacinths the first week if possible. Plant tulips in the first week.

NOVEMBER

1865 It was reported that Izet Williams of Barnstaple was charged with fortune-telling.

❧ 22 ❦

1558 Elizabeth was proclaimed Queen at Exeter in the morning and the Mayor and aldermen in their scarlet gowns with the Council 'in decent and best array' processed to Cathedral Yard and back 'in solemn order'.

1594 Death of Sir Martin Frobisher, soldier and explorer, at Plymouth.

1762 Burial of William Martyn, a Plymouth medical doctor, at Botus Fleming and inscribed on his monument, which stands in a field, was he 'had no superstitious veneration for Church or Churchyard ground, and willing by his example if that might have any influence to lessen the unreasonable esteem which some poor men and women, through prejudice or education, often show for it in frequently parting with the earnings of many a hard Day's Labour, which might be better bestowed in sustenance for themselves and families, to pay for Holy Beds for their Kins-folks' corpses, through a Ridiculous Fear lest their Kins-folks at the Day of Judgement should some way or other suffer because their corpses were wrongly situated or not, where the worldly advantage of their spiritual guides loudly called for them'.

1831 It was reported in Exeter that a false report had appeared in the *Globe* regarding the burning of an effigy of the Bishop.

1948 Six boys, aged between 11 and 14, were fine five shillings each for stealing two holly bushes in Heavitree for their bonfire on the 5th of November.

This is the best month for making alterations in the flower garden, which has now quite lost its beauty. ❋ 1907 – *Early peas and beans may be sown in a*

NOVEMBER

❧ 23 ❦

Astrological Sign of SAGITTARIUS, the Archer
(through to November 23rd)

1791   Baptism at Witheridge of Mary Wilcocks (later Princess Caraboo of Javasu), the daughter of Thomas, shoemaker and Mary, 'almsperson'.

1809   Thirteen patients were discharged from Devon & Exeter Hospital of whom eight were cured of their ailments.

1821   An ice storm at Dartmouth shattered more than 2,500 panes of glass.

1824   Extensive floods were caused by a storm of thunder, lightning and heavy rain with Sidmouth particularly suffering.

1846   An elderly woman died suddenly while dressing to go to a sale at Teignmouth.

1934   Twenty gannets were seen off Brixham harbour.

❧ 24 ❦

1625   It was reported from Plymouth that a snowstorm caused the deaths of many people and had never before 'covered so thick the face of Devon'.

1631   Devon grain prices were reasonably priced given the national shortage.

1814   An attempted balloon flight from the Citadel in Plymouth was abandoned when it struck the spikes around the statue of George II but the balloon escaped and vanished into the clouds.

1817   An apple tree in Colebrook was in full blossom.

warm border; if neglected, most vegetables recommended in September and October may still be planted and earthed up, care being taken to protect them

NOVEMBER

❧ 25 ❧
St Catherine's Day

1503 Nine pence was collected at St Saviour's church, Dartmouth, for pardons.

1549 The annual rental for a Heavitree property was fixed at one red rose.

1814 The balloon missing from Plymouth the previous day was found in the morning near Bridport in Dorset.

1821 Thorverton flooded: furniture in the vicarage's ground floor floated through the rooms and the Dolphin's malt house washed away.

❧ 26 ❧

1560 William Came, Exeter apprentice, was examined before the Mayor for saying in a shop that he wished Queen Elizabeth dead in order that 'the religion should change'.

1825 The fronts of several houses near the Bridge in Exeter were besmeared with coal tar by some 'mischievous characters'.

1881 The Plymouth Lifeboat was called out into the Sound during a heavy storm.

1949 A white fox was seen at Leather Tor Bridge on Dartmoor.

❧ 27 ❧

1627 A storm destroyed two navy ships at Plymouth.

1665 A dog whipper was appointed at Newton St Petrock.

1792 The *Macaroni, Pullen, Nancy, Worthylake, Capelin, Norton, Sally* and the *Champion* arrived in Dartmouth from Newfoundland.

from frost. Force seakale, asparagus, and rhubarb. Prune and plant bushes and fruit trees, and finish flowering trees and shrubs. Transplant seedling stocks

NOVEMBER

❧ 28 ❧

1836   A storm caused widespread damage to buildings and trees.

1916   Knapman of Exeter had on sale Ladies Coats, '270 coats, latest styles, no two alike in colours nigger, grey, wine, navy, purple, heather, saxe, bottle & black'.

1919   Lady Nancy Astor was elected MP for Sutton Division of Plymouth and became the first woman to sit in the House of Commons.

❧ 29 ❧

1564   Sir John Hawkins slaved at Cape Verde where the crew found 'the people are all black and are called Negroes without any apparel, saving before their privates, of stature goodly men'.

1599   Burial of 'Old Mother Stone a midwife' in Dartmouth.

1765   Benjamin Donn was given an award by the Society for the Encouragement of Arts, Manufactures and Commerce for his map of Devon.

1918   A house-to-house collection was held for the Exeter Wounded Soldiers Christmas Fund.

❧ 30 ❧

1653   Thomas Larkham, the troubled vicar of Tavistock, wrote in his diary that William Hodge's wife gave him a fat goose 'Lord, do them good!'.

1846   John West was found stealing plants from the Camelia House of Messrs. Lucombe, Pince and Co. of St Thomas.

1881   Ripe wild strawberries were picked from a hedge in Ashburton.

and suckers taken from the roots of the pear, plum, codling, and quince trees, to prepare them for budding, or grafting different fruits upon. ✲✲✲

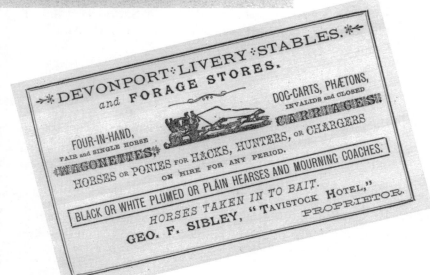

DECEMBER

O dirty December,
For Christmas remember.

Thomas Tusser, 1557

DECEMBER

❧ 1 ❦

1583 The Halberton tax collectors accepted, in lieu of money, a dish of butter, pieces of bacon, half a cheese, one peck of oats and 'some' eggs and 'girts'.

1676 Eight chimneys were swept at Sydenham for one shilling and four pence.

1858 John Gibbs was sentenced to six months' imprisonment with hard labour for stealing six Exminster ducks.

❧ 2 ❦

Birthday of Abraham Cann, Champion Devon Wrestler: born at Colebrook, 1794.

1527 Funeral in Tiverton of Princess Katherine, 'daughter, sister and aunt of Kings', whose coffin was covered with gold cloth decorated with a silver tissue cross and coats of arms. Mourners wore black hoods and gowns and carried banners depicting saints. It was claimed that 8,000 poor people each received two pence on the condition they prayed for her soul.

1755 Fire destroyed the second lighthouse situated on the Eddystone.

1918 The Exeter Union of Carters went on strike.

❧ 3 ❦

Birthday of the Reverend Robert Stephen Hawker: born at Stoke Damerel, 1803

1789 *Hamlet* was performed in Newton Abbot.

❋❋❋ 1891 – *Prepare for future garden operations by digging, manuring, or trenching vacant ground, and collecting leaves, manure, and turf, to make*

DECEMBER

1908 Mr Herbert Booth, youngest son of General Booth of the Salvation Army, gave a lecture in Tiverton on 'Fundamental and Experimental Christianity' as part of his Evangelistic Mission.

1918 Devon men stationed in France thanked the mayor of Exeter for gifts of playing cards and footballs.

1942 A gift auction of live farm stock and produce at Tavistock Cattle Market (for the Red Cross Agriculture Fund) raised £525 including £3 1s for one lemon, £2 for two bananas and £6 for a pair of ducks.

❧ 4 ❧

1732 Death of John Gay, celebrated poet from Barnstaple.

1810 A debtor, petty offender and 2 foreigners were housed in Barnstaple Gaol and Bridewell.

1833 It was reported that 12 sons of north Devon farmers were joining the navy in Plymouth because of the poor state of farming.

❧ 5 ❧

1681 Edmund Tremayne of Collacombe paid Harry fourteen shillings and five pence for shoeing horses and Guscott received two shillings for bleeding and drenching them.

1824 A 'scallop-toed' sandpiper was seen at Sidmouth.

1830 A liver-coloured pointer dog named Riege was missing between Haldon and Kennford.

1835 A river lamprey was caught off Oreston.

compost. In mild weather sow a few radishes and peas in a warm border, and small salads and cucumbers in hotbeds. Cover with straw, fern, litter, or mats,

DECEMBER

❧ 6 ❧

Birthday of George Monk, Duke of Albemarle: born at either Bideford or Great Potheridge, 1608

1601   A week after the burial of one 'blackmore' another, described as 'Mary at Mr Stallenge', was also buried at Plymouth.

1782 (6th–10th)   Chagford's rector was accused of brawling in church.

1831   A rare honeysuckle, the *Xylosteum* or otherwise known as the Upright Honeysuckle, was reported to be found in Bickham Wood near Exeter.

1976   It was suggested that the sonic booms heard at 9.05 pm were caused by blasting operations in the Dunchideock Treacle Mines.

❧ 7 ❧

1602   John Willoughby the elder of Payhembury explained he could identify a particular haggard [wild] Barberry falcon by, among other things, his yellow feet and beak and the silver hawk-rings with the owner's name engraved with a ship's stern.

1650   John Willoughby the younger of Payhembury paid eleven servants their wages and purchased a clock key, bed cord, pound of wick yarn, carrots, turnips and two 'piss pots'.

1847   The members of the Exeter Scientific and Literary Institution heard a lecture on 'The Geography of Plants'.

1942   Jack Benny featured in *Charley's American Aunt* at the Carlton Cinema in Okehampton.

1951   It was reported that holly-hunters had arrived in East Devon to find few berries on plants.

any plants that are liable to be injured by frost, either in frames or in the open ground, admitting free supplies of air when the weather is favourable. Plant

DECEMBER

❧ 8 ❧

1502 The coroner determined that at eleven o'clock at night John Croste stabbed Robert Mathew, Plymouth fisherman, in the stomach with the assistance of Mathew's wife Elizabeth.

1617 Robert Doddridge was accused of contempt of court by saying of the Chancellor that he 'cared not a dog's turd' and 'you may pack up your libel and wipe your arse with it' as well as boasting 'I will, Sir Reverence, make you sh*t worse than wax'.

1766 At night a live cat was tied to the door knocker of a Tiverton apothecary who woke up to the 'hideous and uncommon noise' and cried out to the supposed ghost 'In the name of God why troublest me?' who responded 'P-A-Y thy Brother's debts and legacies, otherwise tor-men-ted thou will be'.

1792 An effigy of Thomas Payne was pelted and then burnt at Plymouth.

1818 Gardens in Plymouth had in full bloom jonquils, narcissus, hyacinths, anemones, pinks, stocks, African and French marigolds, and roses.

1908 Mr Herbert Booth, youngest son of General Booth of the Salvation Army, gave his bioscopic lecture 'The Entrancing Story of the Early Christians' at Tiverton which was 'exquisitely illustrated by 200 life-model and 1,200 feet of animated pictures' which was advertised as 'intensely realistic but in no sense revolting'.

❧ 9 ❧

1615 At the time of his death Michael Harte, Exeter bookseller, owned some 4,558 books worth more than £100.

and prune all sorts of bushes and trees, being careful to stake the trees which are newly planted. In pruning roses, remove the old wood and curtail the young

DECEMBER

Meat was roasted in
Barnstaple in 1676
because it was
reportedly so cold
that water could not
be found to cook
with.

Dense fogs
throughout the
month in 1871.

Exceeds her as much
in beauty as the first
of May doth the last
of December.
William
Shakespeare,
Much Ado About
Nothing, Act I,
Scene 1.

1864 A Sidmouth resident picked several large ripe strawberries in his garden.

1880 Medals were given in Plymouth for soliders who had served in the Zulu War.

1920 At a Special Devonian Service held in London the twenty most distinguished Devonians were named as Saint Boniface, Walter de Stapledon, John de Grandisson, William Courtenay, Sir John Fortescue, Sir John Hawkins, Sir Humphrey Gilbert, Sir Francis Drake, Sir Richard Grenville, Sir Thomas Bodley, Sir Walter Ralegh, George Monk, Duke of Malborough, Thomas Newcomen, Sir Joshua Reynolds, Samuel Taylor Coleridge, J.M.W. Turner, Charles Kingsley, Frederick Temple and Captain Robert Falcon Scott.

❧ 10 ❧

1635 William Lane of Barnstaple was accused of saying of his neighbour Elizabeth Forbes 'thou art cursed out of the church for burning John Witheridge his ***** and guts' and that she was the last woman he 'did commit the act with or **** or occupy & that she was hot as all the ovens in the town'.

1664 A 'blazing star' was seen at Tavistock at four in the morning.

1698 An agreement was made with a Winchester man for renovations to Exeter haven.

1849 At Bridford a rare bird, the Spoonbill, was identified within a flock of geese, then shot and exhibited in Exeter.

1875 Teignmouth's skating rink was covered with a wooden roof and reopened.

1948 The director of the BBC in Plymouth announced it would be five years before television came to the West Country.

straggling branches. ✽ 1896 – *All winter crops of vegetables should be kept free from dead leaves. Decayed flowers should be cut down. Dig the borders,*

DECEMBER

❧ 11 ❧

1624   Six Padstow men drowned sailing over the bar at Barnstaple and were buried at Northam.

1810   The curate of Brixham was absolved of brawling in church.

1826   The King's Arms were carved and gilded by Mr Lascelles in the gallery of St Mary Arches church, Exeter.

1826   It was regretted in *The Alfred – West of England Journal* that a shop front in Fore Street in Exeter (remarkable for the 'successive projection of the stories') was not recorded by an artist before the recent fire.

1830   The Aurora Borealis was seen at Torquay before midnight and several inches of snow fell on Dartmoor.

1936   The Garage in Holwsorthy offered the Popular Ford Saloon, which was 'already the world's most famous light car', at the price of £100.

❧ 12 ❧

1676   Winter began at Plymouth with a cold strong north wind and a sharp frost with snow.

1825   Mr Cross of Fore Street in Exeter placed on show a chicken liver which weighed ten and one half ounces.

1864   A wild cat, measuring thirty inches in length, was caught in Moretonhampstead.

1875   Hospital Sunday in Exeter.

1920 (12th–13th)   More than a foot of snow fell at Salcombe.

taking particular care not to injure any bulbs. Proceed with pruning and nailing whenever an opportunity arises. Inspect the fruit in the store-room at regular

DECEMBER

❧ 13 ❧

1557 The amount of time politicians could speak in Exeter was discussed and it was decided that every member could 'offer and mind to speak on any matter' without interruption except at the mayor's discretion who could stop anyone speaking 'too tedious, too long or to small effect'.

1701 The weekly diet for the Exeter workhouse was established. On Sundays children were allowed:

> At breakfast 3 ounces of bread, 1 ounce of cheese, ½ pint of beer
>
> At dinner 4 ounces of bread, 8 ounces of beef, 1 pint of beer, sufficient garden 'stuff'
>
> At supper 4 ounces of bread, 1½ ounces of cheese or 1 ounce of butter, ½ pint of beer

1809 It was announced in *Woolmer's Exeter and Plymouth Gazette* that in Exeter 'according to the rites and ceremonies of the Jewish persuasion' Mr J. Jacobs was married to Miss E. Levy.

1942 Professor Arthur Newell, advertised as the man Haw-Haw called 'that man Newell', gave a talk entitled 'America Faces the War' at South Molton Cinema.

❧ 14 ❧

1594 Burial of Roger Swinsbury of Plymouth who died of plague as did his two sons and wife in the previous four weeks.

1677 A dispute over the employment of teachers at Honiton Grammar School ended with a license to William Knight. Ambrose Cleake, a fellow teacher who taught English, writing and arithmetic, had objected that Knight was a 'phanatick' and that there were insufficient pupils to support them.

and frequent intervals, and remove whatever is found to be in a state of decay.
Protect beds of tulips, hyacinths, &c. ✱ 1898 – *Sow a few beans and peas as in*

DECEMBER

1792 *The Merchant of Venice* was performed at Dartmouth.

1875 It was reported that Zaida and Moltke II of Tiverton won prizes in the Swansea Dog Show.

1918 Devon women, those aged at least 30, voted for the first time.

1936 A 'Rat Month' was proposed at Braunton to deal with the 'fine great rats, like cats, mooching around'.

❧ 15 ❧

1531 Thomas Bennet, who had been arrested at Exeter on suspicion of heresy, was ordered to be burnt 'for his opinions'.

1821 A spaniel and rabbit fell into a mine shaft and although the dog was rescued, the rabbit was killed by the fall.

1876 Madame Bradnee Rinaldi's select classes on Dancing, Deportment and Calisthenics were advertised at Torquay, Dartmouth, Plymouth, Bideford, Ilfracombe, Barnstaple, Exeter, Newton Abbot, Devonport and Teignmouth.

❧ 16 ❧

1846 Gatcombe Bailey won First Prize in 'Improvement in Writing' in the awards given at Bedford Circus School, Exeter.

1847 The Devon Hounds met at Parke in Bovey Tracey and the Tiverton Fox Hounds at Beechcombe in Skilgate.

1989 A hurricane hit the south of England, causing great destruction in Devon.

November. Very few operations can be carried on this month with the exception of trenching and digging in dry weather, operations which should by all means

DECEMBER

❧ 17 ❧

1585 The Mayor of Exeter ordered twelve pence be given to the bear baiter.

1823 A storm pulled down chimneys in Exeter and caused great damage to Dittisham church.

1825 A wrestling match was suggested between the Cornish Champion, James Polkinghorne, and Abraham Cann, the Devon Champion.

1826 Death of Sarah Catherine Martin, creator of Old Mother Hubbard.

❧ 18 ❧

1792 A rally was held in Plymouth to support the King.

1821 It was reported in Exeter that an eighteen-year old girl died of fright after one of her schoolmates threw a spider at her.

1936 The Mayor of Exeter, the 'Ever Faithful' city, pledged loyalty to King George VI.

❧ 19 ❧

1676 Cold weather persisted at Plymouth with a north wind and 'the season continues very sharp as the like has not been in these parts these many years'.

1827 The Devon Fox Hunters' Club met at Bycott.

1876 In Exeter 'Rich Real Seal Skin Jackets' were available as Christmas presents.

be attended to. The ground should be thoroughly well turned up for exposure to the frost and snow. Plant all sorts of fruit-trees in mild weather. Proceed with

DECEMBER

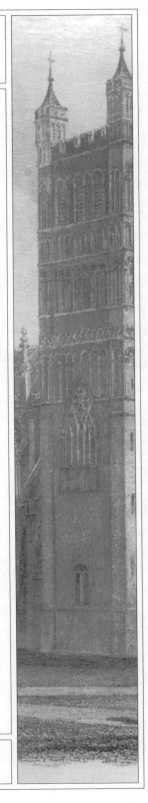

❧ 20 ❧

1784 At Saltram 38,000 trees were about to be planted.

1823 It was reported that workmen digging in Butcher Row in Exeter found a Roman medal which allegedly had the likeness of Napoleon.

1830 William Yard, accused in Exeter of deserting his wife, was described as 'literally a yard of bad stuff'.

1882 Trials were held of the *Sapphire*, 12 screw corvette, outside the Plymouth Breakwater.

❧ 21 ❧

1523 The abbot of Forde sent the Countess of Devon a boar and two swans for her Christmas celebrations.

1763 Fire destroyed a printer's shop in Larkbeare.

1810 Lightning struck the steeple of Barnstaple parish church.

1833 It was reported that an Anemone was in full blossom in Mr Webber's garden in St Sidwell.

❧ 22 ❧

1635 The Mayor of Plymouth reported a fight of a dozen Dutch sailors, knives, swords and several men being stabbed in the stomach and back.

1821 Growing on a tree at Annery near Bideford were apples reputedly the size of pigeon's eggs.

1870 The coldest day of the year in Jacobstowe at 14° and also one of the coldest at Great Torrington.

pruning and nailing wall trees. ✻ *1900 – Trenching, digging, and riding may proceed if the ground is not too well. In mild weather transplanting and*

DECEMBER

1931 The County Council discussed the controversial subject of siting petrol pumps.

❧ 23 ❧

Astrological Sign of CAPRICORN, the Goat
(through to January 20th)

1669 Burial of the Reverend Thomas Larkham, vicar of Northam and Tavistock, whose reputation for controversy was due to inflammatory remarks to parishioners ('squint-eye fools and ninihammers'), a fondness for tobacco and alcohol, and a sudden departure from New England after an accusation of bastardy.

1879 It was announced that children occupying seats would pay full fare on Plymouth tram cars.

1918 D.W. Griffith's war romance *Hearts of the World* played at Victoria Hall in Exeter.

1920 Snow began to melt at Salcombe after ten days.

❧ 24 ❧
Christmas Eve

1592 Gonzalo Gonzales del Castillo, a prisoner since the defeat of the Armada four years before, sailed from Exeter for Britanny.

1670 The rector of Hittisleigh was forced to renounce saying, in church, that the 'sins of England were greater than the sins of Sodom and Gomorrah' and that the fire of London was a judgement upon England.

pruning may be performed, and in frosty weather manure to on to the ground. Keep all winter crops free from dead leaves. Potatoes and onions may be planted

DECEMBER

1821 A Stonehouse constable assaulted a young man in an attempt to stop carol singing.

1827 It was reported that ripe strawberries were picked in a Combe Martin garden.

1837 A flock of swallows were seen at Berry Head.

1839 A low rumble of noise was heard early in the morning at Dowlands Farm near Axmouth.

1865 A disturbance resulted after the Beaford church choir collected money for singing Christmas carols: one member was bitten on the thumb, another had his face scratched and the third had a pair of black eyes.

1936 Gracie Fields featured in *Queen of Hearts* at The Cinema, Holsworthy.

1943 Tyrone Power featured in *Son of Fury* at The Cinema, Holsworthy.

1948 Robert Lowery featured in *God's Country* at The Cinema, Holsworthy.

❧ 25 ❧
Quarter Day Christmas

1285 King Edward I and Queen Eleanor visit Exeter.

1533 The Ashburton churchwardens gave two shillings as a reward and allowance 'to the players of a Christmas game that played in the said church'.

1652 John Taylor, the water-poet, visited Devon where one farmer 'with the dame of the house and everybody else were exceeding glad to see me. With all country courtesy and solemnity, I was had into the parlour. There I was placed at

any time during the month when the ground is dry. Cut down any decayed flowers and dig the borders, taking care not to injure the bulbs. ✦ 1901 – *All*

DECEMBER

the upper end of the table and my company about me. We had good cheer and free welcome and we were merry without music. After dinner we arose from the board and sat by the fire – where the hearth was embroidered all over with roasted apples, piping hot, expecting a bowl of ale for a cooler (which presently was transformed into warm lambswool). Within an hour after we went to church we returned home where we discoursed merrily, without either profaneness or obscenity; supper being ended we went to cards; some sung carols and merry songs (suitable to the times) then the poor labouring hinds and the maid-servants, with the plough-boys, went nimbly to dancing, the poor toiling wretches being all glad of my company because they had little or no sport at all till I came amongst them and therefore they leaped and skipped for joy, singing a catch to the tune of "HEY":

> *Let's dance and sing, and make good cheer,*
> *For Christmas comes but once a year.*

Thus at active games and gambols of hot-cockles, shoeing the wild mare and the like harmless sports, some part of the night was spent'.

1814   Several inches of snow fell at night in Exeter.

1825   A large double stock was picked from a florist's garden in Tavistock.

1828   John Green, 17, stole a handkerchief from a gentleman's pocket (and was subsequently transported overseas for 14 years).

1837   An Exeter tradesman, who was jokingly told his son had died, fell into a tremor and died three months later.

1839   Rumbling noises were again heard early in the morning at Dowlands Farm near Axmouth preceding the fall of some eight million tons of earth in the Great Landslip – ¾ mile long, 300 feet wide and 150 feet deep.

winter crops of vegetables should be kept free from dead leaves. Decayed flowers should be cut down. Dig the borders, taking particular care not to injure any

DECEMBER

1846 Roast beef, plum pudding and strong beer were served to the inmates of Exeter gaol.

1852 The *Ocean Queen* was wrecked on the Plymouth Mew Stone.

1874 Beef, vegetables, plum pudding and beer was served to the inmates of the Bideford Workhouse. Oranges, raisins and nuts followed.

1927 (25th–26th) Heavy snow fell across Devon with more than a foot on Dartmoor.

❧ 26 ❧

Birthday of Charles Babbage, mathematician: born at Walworth, Surrey, 1791.

1590 The *Prudence* of Barnstaple arrived at Appledore with a Portuguese ship captured on the African coast. It had the highest value then seen in Barnstaple including 4 chests of gold (valued at £16,000) but the total worth was incalculable due to pillage by the crew.

1683 Eight pence was spent on an ounce of 'Spanish flys' at Sydenham.

1839 Visitors began arriving at Dowlands Farm near Axmouth to see the Great Landslip.

1846 A quail was shot in Exminster marshes.

❧ 27 ❧

1815 Death of Joanna Southcott, visionary, in London.

1823 Small pox was prevalent in Kingsbridge.

bulbs. Proceed with pruning and nailing whenever an opportunity arises. Inspect the fruit in the store-room at regular and frequent intervals, and remove whatever

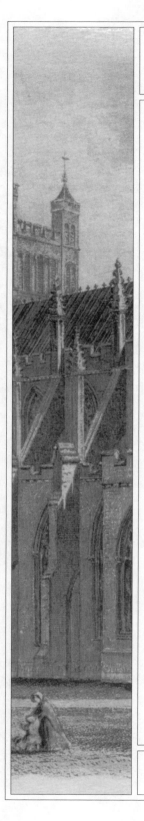

DECEMBER

1831 Charles Darwin left Plymouth on HMS *Beagle* for its five-year scientific survey.

1833 Woodcocks in Exeter Market sold at five shillings per couple and snipes were two shillings a brace.

1877 The local Christey Minstrel Troupe at Dolton included Mr James Hodge (singing 'The Colorado Beetle'), Mr A. Risdon ('Pretty little girl with the tight boot on') and Mr. W. Weekes in female costume ('Betsy Wareing').

1962 Six inches or more of snow fell over east and south Devon.

☙ 28 ❧
Innocents' Day Childermas

***c.*1611** John Willoughby of Payhembury invited 13 guests for supper and the food was probably similar to an earlier menu of 1 capon and broth, 3 pieces of boiled beef, 2 pieces of roast beef, 4 minced pies, 1 goose, 1 pig, 1 loin of veal, 2 lambs, 1 loin of baked mutton with a second course being 2 caponets, 2 rabbits, 2 chickens, 2 custard pies, 2 apple pies and 2 pear pies.

1847 Croydon's Celebrated Anti-Bug Composition (and Lotion for Destroying House Bugs) was on sale by George Owen, Exeter druggist.

1877 A dead whale washed ashore at Westward Ho!

☙ 29 ❧

1628 Plymouth's mayor ordered that George Elliot, mariner, be given the gold ring, silver beaker, 4 silver spoons and whistle held since his wife died of plague.

---

is found to be in a state of decay. Protect beds of tulips, hyacinths, &c. ✤ *1907 – Prepare for future garden operations by digging, manuring or trenching vacant*

DECEMBER

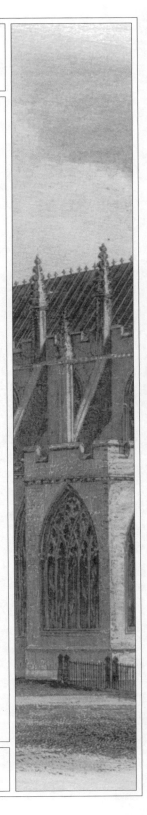

1763 Gossip in Holsworthy centred on a local gentleman who, two months after his father's death, announced that he had been married to his father's housekeeper for ten years.

1865 Complaints were made in Sidmouth of the 'Mummer and Mumster Nuisance' whereby parties of boys and men, sometimes masked, caused mischief at night.

1876 Among those attending a fancy dress ball at Teignmouth were Lady Help, Mother Hubbard, Lady of the 19th Century, Canada, Roman Peasant, Kate the Shrew, Dick Turpin, Garibaldian Volunteer, Cricketer, Jockey, Sailor and French Farmer. Dancing began on roller skates.

1899 In *The Devon Weekly Times* the mild weather and lack of snow was compared with previous years.

❧ 30 ❧

1619 Burial at Topsham of an unnamed 'poor boy' of whom no more is known.

1752 Burial of Walter Pyke of Bere Ferrers on whose memorial stone was inscribed:

> *By a fall I caught my death*
> *Which no man knows his time nor breath*
> *I might have died as soon as then*
> *Had I been with physician men.*

1874 About 200 quarts of soup were served at the Exeter Soup Kitchen.

1899 The Pantomime *Cinderella* played at Exeter's Theatre Royal to rave reviews.

1944 Abbot and Costello appeared in *Lost in a Harem* at the Savoy in Exeter.

ground and collecting leaves, turf and manure to make compost. In mild weather sow a few radishes and peas in a warm border and small salads and cucumbers

DECEMBER

❧ 31 ❦

1788 There were fears in Dartmouth for more than 100 ships not home from Newfoundland.

1814 More than 3,000 American prisoners were held at Princetown.

1843 Awliscombe's vicar gave a ball and supper for more than 100 parishioners and local gentry in the school room decorated with festoons of evergreens and banners.

1846 The railway reached Newton Abbot.

1851 A Great Bustard was shot in Bratton Clovelly.

1852 Opening of the Devonport Sailors' Home.

1872 Children were accused of plundering East Budleigh churchyard of its snowdrops.

1899 The Editor of *The Devon Weekly Times* wrote the year had been one of national humiliation in contrast to previous years and reflected on the imminent arrival of the new century. He noted he was 'far, very far from the Millennium of the Poet' who wrote

> *Ring out the narrow lust of gold*
> *Ring out the thousand wars of old*
> *Ring in the thousand years of peace.*

in hot beds. Cover with straw, any plants that are liable to be injured by frost, admitting free supplies of fresh air when the weather is favourable. ✱✱✱

Directory, Office, South St Exeter.

205]

IDENTIFICATION OF
MARGINAL ILLUSTRATIONS

❧ ❀❀❀ ☙

Pages 1–31. *Watermouth, near Ilfracombe, Devonshire.* Steel engraving published by P. Jackson, London, 1849. (Westcountry Studies Library, SC 101)

Pages 33–58. *Torquay, from Park Terrace.* Lithograph published by G. Rowe, Cheltenham, *c.* 1845. (Westcountry Studies Library, SC 3221)

Pages 60–85. *The Sound, Breakwater Mount Edgecumbe, from Mutton Cove.* Lithograph published by W. Byers and S. Saunders, Devonport, *c.* 1830. (Westcountry Studies Library, SC 2263)

Pages 87–118. *Devonport from Mount Edgecumbe.* Steel engraving published by J. and W. Robins, London, 1856 for the *Stationer's Almanack*. (Westcountry Studies Library, SC 1970)

Pages 121–146. *Northernhay, Exeter, looking over St David's.* Lithograph published by Spreat and Wallis, Exeter, *c.* 1845. (Westcountry Studies Library, SC 147)

Pages 148–168. *Exeter, from Exwick Fields*. Steel engraving by Paterson and Fenn. Late-19th century. (private collection)

Pages 171–191. *Haldon House, Kenn*. Lithograph of 1892. (Devon Record Office, 3860/E1)

Pages 193–205. *Exeter Cathedral*. Steel engraving published by H. Besley, Exeter, *c.* 1860. (Westcountry Studies Library, SC 227)